THE LONG WAY HOME

James R. Schultz

THE LONG WAY HOME

A Pacific Odyssey of World War II

CREATIVE ARTS BOOK CO.
BERKELEY · 1996

The Long Way Home is published by Donald S. Ellis
and distributed by Creative Arts Book Company.

For Information contact:
Creative Arts Book Company
833 Bancroft Way
Berkeley, California 94710

ISBN 0-88739-114-1
Library of Congress Catalog Number 96-84603

Printed in the United States of America

The cover photo was taken from the spectacular pyrotechnic display which erupted from the
2,000 ships assembled in Leyte Gulf on August 10, 1945 with news of the Japanese surrender.

To Dorothy

Acknowledgements

This book would not have been possible without access to my father's collection of the letters I had written to him and other family members during World War II. With information gleaned from the letters and my recollection of events, substantiated by Navy records and conversations with other officers, I was able to reconstruct my four years of experience in the Navy. The project originated as a personal memoir intended only for family members, but with the encouragement of family and friends it developed into a story suitable for publication.

I am indebted to Charlotte and Bob Hockett who recommended that I submit the manuscript to Creative Arts Book Company. There are many other people who have been helpful along the way, but I want particularly to acknowledge my former skipper, Art Bergstrom, John Bohn, Joe Campana, Dave Robertson, Paul Sciranka, Ray Shafer, and Bob Tiernan. Invaluable assistance has also been provided by my wife Dorothy, my daughter Margaret Blair, and my editor Don Ellis whose guidance and wise counsel has nurtured the project to fruition.

C O N T E N T S

Foreword

While a student at Allegheny College I developed a great respect and affection for Dr. John Richie Schultz, who as a professor and Dean of Men at the time, provided me with wise counsel and support. I was among many Allegheny graduates with whom Dr. Schultz corresponded regularly during World War II. Having grown up in the same community of Meadville, Pennsylvania, I have known his son Jim for many years. Jim was a freshman at Allegheny during my senior year and we later crossed paths on a remote island in the South Pacific when we were both in the Navy. After the war we pursued careers in different parts of the country and saw each other only on rare occasions. It was a pleasant surprise then to learn that Jim had undertaken to chronicle his Navy experience in World War II. When he sent me a copy of his manuscript I was immediately intrigued.

As a former Navy officer and active participant in the Allied drive to rout the Japanese from their Pacific island strongholds, I was able to identify with the author's fascinating account of his experience. His stories and anecdotes, drawn from the day to day lives of the officers and crew of the ships on which he served, held my interest from start to finish, recalling my own tour of duty in the South Pacific. His narrative captures the experience and emotions of many of us who served in the Pacific theater of World War II. He describes the excitement, the boredom, the humor and fears of life at sea in a world at war. He writes with clarity and attention to detail that reflects a remarkable ability to recall names, places, and events which took place many years ago. His book will be of interest not only to those of us who served in World War II but also to others who would like to gain more insight into this significant chapter of our nation's history. I know that the reader will thoroughly enjoy this excellent book.

Raymond Philip Shafer
former Governor of Pennsylvania

Prologue

The seeds of World War II were planted in the early 1920's when an obscure demagogue named Adolph Hitler surfaced on Germany's political scene. Hitler had been imprisoned for a short time in 1923 after an aborted effort to overthrow the government. He emerged from prison more determined than ever and founded the Fascist Party, a political faction which grew rapidly in the economic chaos following World War I. It developed into a strong nationalistic movement, capitalizing on the general unrest of the poverty stricken masses. By 1933 the Fascists had become strong enough for Hitler to maneuver the German Reichstag into passing legislation which gave him absolute dictatorial power. He continued to consolidate his power under the Nazi banner until his troops were able to occupy the German Rhineland and later Austria in 1938. By that time his war machine had reached a peak of strength and efficiency.

The next target in his ruthless march through Europe was Sudetenland, a former province of Austria which had been ceded to Czechoslovakia under terms of the Treaty of Versailles at the end of World War I. Under the pretext of liberating the largely German population Hitler convinced both France and England to step aside while his troops swept into Sudetenland. The Munich Agreement, signed by Prime Ministers Dadalier of France and Chamberlain of Great Britain, was the infamous pact which sealed the fate of that vulnerable piece of geography. It also led Hitler to believe that the major powers would not intercede as he prepared to seize other countries. He marched almost unopposed into the rest of Czechoslovakia in March of 1939. When that happened Neville Chamberlain announced that appeasement had come to end. Hitler soon declared war on Poland which prompted England and France to declare war on Germany. Hitler's Panzer Divisions swept through the low countries and World War II was in full flower.

The mood in the United States was still pacifist, a reaction to the horrors of World War I. Public policy was still isolationist. Alert to concerns about the Nazi drive across Europe, President Franklin Roosevelt articulated a world view designed to arouse the public conscience. To students at Allegheny College in 1939 the war was remote. The homecoming football game against Grove City was more exciting. As the news trickled in from Europe some uneasiness was expressed, but it was easy to dismiss such thoughts when the snow hung heavy on the tall pine trees and the rhododendrons bloomed in the campus ravine.

In the old Huidekoper mansion which had become the Phi Delta Theta fraternity house, a group of us sat comfortably in front of the massive hand-carved wooden fireplace in the reception hall. Warmed by a roaring fire we speculated on what could be only an outside chance that the United States would be drawn into the war. What could we do? How would we react? Was there a way to avoid military service? The perfect solution was presented and we all agreed. We would charter a yacht, sail for unidentified islands in the South Pacific, and cruise under balmy skies until the war was over. Having made that portentious decision, we tuned in to the Hit Parade on KDKA Radio.

It hadn't occurred to us that a Japanese menace was in our future. On December 7, 1941 the Japanese, having joined Germany to establish a second front, bombed Pearl Harbor in a surprise attack that shocked the nation. The United States reacted immediately and declared war on both countries. The rules of the game had changed. No longer were we pacifists calmly viewing a distant war. In a burst of patriotism many of us who by that time were in graduate school entered the military service. I applied for a Naval Officer's commission the day after Pearl Harbor and went on active duty as an Ensign in May of 1942. My seagoing saga is recounted in the pages which follow.

THE LONG WAY HOME

War Comes To The Oregon Coast

It was a swift transition from the hallowed halls of academe to the discipline of life at sea in a world at war. Within days after leaving graduate school I was thrust into an accelerated 60 day training program at the U.S. Naval Reserve Midshipmen's School on the downtown campus of Northwestern University. It was at best a crash course in the text book basics of seamanship, designed for landlubbers like me. Having grown up in land-locked Crawford County, Pennsylvania, my sea-going credentials were slim. Rowing a boat on Conneaut Lake is a dubious qualification for a line officer of the Naval Reserve. I learned to navigate with a sextant on the roof of Tower Hall, just off Michigan Avenue in Chicago.

Following Northwestern was a one month stint of post graduate training at the Local Defense School on Treasure Island in San Francisco Bay. It was a regimen of early morning calisthenics, classroom lectures and daytime jaunts on small ships in San Francisco Bay. Most memorable was the sight of Pan American's pioneering China Clippers as they rose from the Bay's choppy waters and soared over the island to disappear in the fog. Completing my formal training was an adventurous six weeks at the Naval Section Base, Coos Bay, Oregon. What was intended as routine on-the-job training turned into total immersion.

Coos Bay was a Navy outpost with a minimal shore-based staff and two 110 foot sub-chasers, the SC-537 and the SC-538. They patrolled the coast from Southern Oregon to Northern California. The base was a lonely, dismal place with spartan accommodations and not much excitement. We rarely saw the sun. The fog rolled in every night and stayed most of the day. The foghorns moaned all night interrupted only by muffled whistles from the fishing boats that sailed in and out of the harbor. The shore based routine was about as dull as routine can be, so I leapt at the chance to spend a week aboard one of the sub-chasers as it crept up and down the fog laden coast. In navigating the coastal waters, caution was the watchword. My week at sea was a lesson in vigilance. After that it was back to paperwork in the base office until an opportunity came along to spend another week at sea aboard the SC-538.

On a quiet Sunday morning in October 1942 a puzzling event occurred about thirty miles offshore. Patrol planes reported that a Standard Oil tanker, the S.S. Camden, was on fire and sinking due west of the Section Base. The two sub-chasers were immediately dispatched to investigate. They found the ship but no trace of survivors. The ship appeared to be an empty burning hull, the victim of a Japanese torpedo. The missile had hit squarely on the bow just below the water line. When first spotted, the bow was underwater with the stern rising at a precarious angle. As the patrol boats continued to watch, the fire subsided and eventually burned out. At that point the commander of our base, Lieutenant Commander (LCDR) W. R. Brust, sprang into action. He was a crusty old salt who had come up through the ranks in the Merchant Marine. He sensed that this could be his moment of glory and he seized the moment. He was going to save the tanker.

The two sub-chasers were guarding the ship, so Commander Brust commandeered a fifty eight foot fishing vessel, the Rio Janeiro, and called for volunteers to join him in the rescue effort. Being young, rash, and bored with shore duty, I signed up with no hesitation. Lt. (jg) T.L. Gerhard, an officer permanently assigned to the base, and eleven enlisted men were the other volunteers. Commander Brust also found two steam fitters from the town of Coos Bay who were willing to come along. We hoped that they could help to start up the ship's engines. As soon as the group could assemble, all sixteen of us trekked down to the dock and boarded the boat. In our hurry to get going, there was no time to pack clothing or other necessities, so I left with only the clothes on my back and a toothbrush I grabbed and put in my pocket.

By Navy standards the fishing boat was miniscule. Two fishermen occupied a small cabin which served as a pilot house with cramped living quarters. The rest of us, including Commander Brust, crowded onto the open fantail, completely at the mercy of the wind and the waves. That night we had plenty of both. The seas were choppy and the waves washed over the fantail, drenching us with cold salty water. To keep warm we pulled a big tarp over us, but much of the time we were hanging over the side, retching and hoping the night would come to an end. It finally did but we still hadn't found 'the tanker. All we had seen during the night was a periscope which made us nervous, but we were left alone. Eventually we located the tanker and climbed up a rope ladder which was conveniently suspended from the deck. Still there was no sign of the Camden's crew.

Before we boarded, Commander Brust issued strict orders: NO SMOKING. The ship's cargo was high octane gasoline! Once on board we began to assess the damage and found that the engine room was flooded. There was no way the ship could proceed under its own power, but Commander Brust was determined. He decided to bring in a tug and tow the ship to Portland. Meanwhile we set up housekeeping and each person was assigned specific responsibilities. The Commander was outraged to find that the Captain of the Camden had left his ship without taking the ship's log. It is a cardinal rule of the sea that the log must be saved when a ship is abandoned. The Commander turned to me and said "Schultz, you're in charge of the log. Make entries every four hours and keep it at all times in your possession." The message registered.

I was also designated to check periodically on the condition of the damaged bow. For obvious reasons I took that job very seriously and made frequent trips back across the catwalk to measure whether and how far the bow had settled into the water. Each day there seemed to be a perceptible change. Most unsettling were the creaks and groans as the damaged bulkheads rubbed against each other. There was always the possibility that a spark could ignite the gasoline.

It took several days for the tug to arrive. Because of the Camden's size and the drag from the sunken bow, we had requested one of the largest seagoing tugs. After the tow was rigged we hoped to make progress on our journey to Portland, but a day later we were still in the same place. That meant that we had to hitch up a second tug which we did when the U.S.S. Shawnee, a more powerful tug, arrived. Meanwhile to protect us from another torpedo attack, a destroyer, the U.S.S. Barker (DD-213), joined the three small subchasers which formed our escort. On Tuesday after our Monday morning boarding we had a submarine scare and the destroyer dropped twelve depth charges. With each blast the tanker shook and groaned more than ever and we worried that either the gasoline would ignite or more bulkheads would give way. By that time the bow had settled an additional two feet. A second destroyer arrived on Wednesday to strengthen the escort flotilla. The Navy was determined to salvage the Camden and fend off any Japanese submarines that may have been lurking in the area. There was the thought that the Japs may have wanted to finish off a job they didn't quite complete.

Once aboard the tanker we tried to make ourselves as comfortable as possible. We had access to the food freezers and storage bins but we couldn't do any cooking. The pantries and refrigerators were well stocked, but the turkeys, chickens, beef and other meat products were beginning to thaw so we talked the escort vessels into stirring up some hot meals for us. They came alongside to pick up the food and brought back hot coffee, beef stew and vegetable soup. Commander Brust showed us another side of his usually brusk personality when he had us put together a huge sign which we hung over the side. It changed daily and read : "BIG SALE — PRIME BEEF" or "PRICES SLASHED — FLOUR AND SUGAR". It attracted the escort vessels which would come alongside and load up with provisions.

The ride aboard the tanker wasn't a picnic but we ate well in picnic style. Sleep was a problem because we were on shifts with four hours on duty and two off. During those two hours we napped pretty well on cots, with warmth from blankets which we found in a bulging linen closet. There was only enough water for drinking and a few necessities like brushing teeth and washing hands and face. Nobody shaved, no baths were allowed and because the toilets didn't work it was over the side for other bathroom functions. For entertainment we rigged up a radio with batteries and a couple of the crew turned out to be fair musicians when we discovered a banjo and a guitar. All of us joined in singing some of the old time tunes. Commander Brust later told the press that our favorite song was " Time On My Hands".

With a more powerful tow we began to make headway at about three knots an hour, still heading for Portland. By Wednesday we could see the Oregon coast, but the winds picked up, the waves were higher, and at one point the tow line parted. Despite the rough seas we were able to secure the tow but decided we could never get across the Columbia River Bar. Our measurements showed that the bow was sinking little by little which meant a deeper draft. Meanwhile, the camp we set up on the stern was rising higher and higher. Instead of back and forth we found ourselves walking up and down at a 35 degree angle. We scratched Portland from the itinerary and hoped we could make it into Seattle.

On the fourth day I continued to make my periodic checks on the bow, but I didn't like what I was seeing. During the afternoon it had gone down several feet in a couple of hours. I reported my concern to Commander Brust but he gave me the stock answer he had been giving me all week: "It's just a following sea." In all that time he had not gone back to get a firsthand look. At 5:30 in the afternoon I finally persuaded him to go and see for himself. As soon as he left I told Ted Gebhard that I thought the ship was going to sink any minute. We both donned life jackets and waited for Commander Brust's reaction. It didn't take long. He came back on the run and hollered "Abandon Ship". We didn't waste any time. We shot off guns, blew whistles, and used semaphore flags to attract attention. The destroyers and subchasers came racing to our side, but the first to arrive was a whaleboat from the tugboat Shawnee. We threw over a rope ladder and scurried down to the relative safety of the pitching whaleboat.

As the crew started to climb over the side I remembered the ship's log. As I ran to get it, the Commander, who had impressed on me the importance of saving the log when a ship is abandoned, yelled "Where are you going?" When I told him he said "To hell with the log. We need to get off this ship." I came running back but I had the ship's log clutched under my arm. When we boarded the Shawnee the first thing we did was head for the showers. Then we devoured the first complete meal we had had in five days. After that the wait began. A watch was posted at the tow lines and the Shawnee's crew was set to sever the lines if the Camden began to go down. All day Friday the Camden stayed afloat. By that time there were three tugs in the tow, the Shawnee, the Mahopac and the Salvage Queen. On Saturday morning at 6:15 A.M. there was a violent explosion and the Camden sank in flames. It was a disappointing end to such a valiant effort.

Ted Gerhard and the eleven enlisted men left the tug on Friday on the SC-537 but Commander Brust and I stayed aboard until after the Camden sank. All of us rendezvoused in Astoria where the newspaper reporters and photographers were waiting. Commander Brust was in his element. He told how we had "walked whistling and singing into the fiery jaws of death". "What a crew!" The newspapers also reported that some of us jumped into the "ice cold waters of the Pacific" when we abandoned ship. None of us did but it made a good story. The real story was that a Japanese submarine had torpedoed an American ship only thirty miles from the Oregon coast. The

Torpedoed tanker S.S. Camden

Volunteer crew which tried in vain to salvage the Camden. I am the sober-faced officer on the left in the front row.

Camden was the third merchant victim of enemy action in the Northern Pacific in less than a year, so the West Coast had reason for concern.

The mystery of the Camden's crew was revealed after all of us were safely ashore. With the ship in flames forty eight survivors had been picked up by a foreign merchant vessel flying a neutral flag. The ship had been hit by three torpedoes, all of which had landed far enough forward that the crew were able to lower life boats. The only casualty was a fifteen year old messboy who was so frightened that he jumped into the ocean and couldn't be rescued.

When we returned to the Section Base Commander Brust issued orders for me to go aboard the U.S.S. SC-538 as Executive Officer, replacing an officer who had been seriously ill and was transferred to a Navy hospital in Seattle. My stint aboard the 538 was short-lived because the Bureau of Naval Personnel had other plans. In short order I was off to a new assignment which eventually took me to the South Pacific.

------◄------◄-----   *Route of the APc-37*
━━━━━◄━━━━━◄━━━━━   *Route of the PC(C)-804*

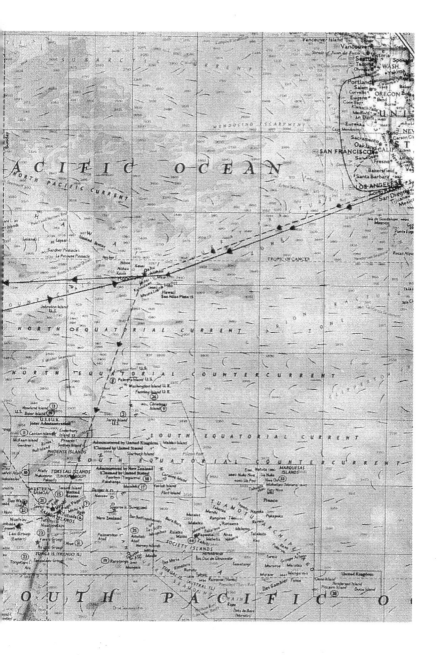

Testing The Waters

The orders read new construction and the place was San Francisco. After four months of training I looked forward to taking my place as a full-fledged line officer, even though it would be weeks before the ship to which I was assigned, the U.S.S. APc-37, would be ready for sea. That time finally came in March 1943 when we sailed under the Golden Gate Bridge on our way to San Pedro. There we joined the other ships of APc Flotilla 5 to embark on the first leg of a long ocean voyage.

As our tiny ship pitched and rolled on its way from San Pedro to Pearl Harbor, reality set in. This was not the romantic escape to the South Seas our group of Phi Delts had in mind when they talked about a safe haven from the perils of war. We were headed for a major theater of World War II and we were cast as participants. It had been fifteen months from the date of the U.S. Declaration of War. In that time the Japanese had occupied not only large areas of China and Southeast Asia but most of the islands of the Western Pacific. They had invaded the islands with thousands of small ships, many of which were commandeered fishing boats similar in design to the APc. What was ahead for the U.S.S. APc-37?

In a sense the word "ship" was a euphemism for our 103 foot "boat". It looked more like an oversized fishing vessel than the commissioned United States warship it really was. Wooden hulled with an oversized super-structure, the APc 37 looked clumsy. It was to be my home for months to come, a thought that did little for my ebbing morale. To my surprise it proved to be remarkably dependable, comfortable and seaworthy. It carried

Checking out my new ship, the APc-37

me through tropical storms and seas so rough that capsizing seemed imminent. During a severe squall the roll was so pronounced that the crew with nervous bravado chanted "Roll over, you son-of-a-bitch". Another time the cook dashed from the galley to tell me that the bag of coffee grounds had just rolled out of the large coffee urn as the ship was rocked by an enormous wave. Many times I blessed the master craftsmen at Anderson and Cristafani Shipyards, one of several small high quality builders engaged by the Navy to construct the APc class of ships.

Anderson and Cristafani, a builder of fishing boats and yachts, was located at Hunters Point in San Francisco close to the Hunters Point Naval Shipyard. As the APc 37 neared completion, its crew gradually assembled and the three officers assigned to the ship reported for duty to check supplies and equipment and prepare for commissioning. Lt. (jg) Art Bergstrom, age 24, was to be the Commanding Officer and Al Farrell, age 23, Executive Officer. Jim Schultz, age 22, youngest of the three , was given multiple responsibilities, including gunnery and engineering. Twenty six enlisted men rounded out the crew of twenty nine. They represented a cross-section of America's melting pot and were a study in contrasts.

Thomas Curtin from Brooklyn was the street-wise urban sophisticate who kept us entertained with his wise-cracks, earthy humor and genuine good nature. He took his responsibilities seriously in the important role of Ship's Cook and kept us gastronomically content. He had a dozen different recipes for Spam, could whip up delicious pancakes for breakfast and prepare tasty grilled fish which we caught as we trolled slowly through South Pacific waters. When I

Officers of the APc-37: Jim Schultz, Art Bergstrom, and Al Farrell

was hospitalized with a 104 degree fever in the Solomon Islands he showed up with a baked potato which was the only thing I wanted to eat. That was a time when most of our potatoes were dehydrated and baking potatoes were hard to come by.

From Louisiana there were Edward Barousse and Clarence Boudreaux whose looks and speech betrayed their Cajun backgrounds. From Nebraska, Arkansas and Oregon were boys who had rarely ventured beyond the boundaries of the farms they were raised on. Curtin insisted that they had to sprinkle cow dung on the gangplank to get them aboard.

Joe DeRose, Seaman First Class, was a bright well-spoken entrepreneur who owned a slot machine business in Syracuse and aspired to be an officer. He drove a big Buick convertible around San Francisco before we left the States and perhaps for that reason was popular with the crew. There was an intriguing rumor, never substantiated, that he came from a Mafia family.

Gunner's Mate Third Class, Olin Chester Morrow, was a twenty two year old from Santa Barbara. He was tough on the surface, but thoughtful and considerate of others. He was one of our most dependable and hard working men and a strong leader.

Salvadore Gonzales, Steward, was a widower from the Philippines with two sons, ages 15 and 16, who remained at his home in Japanese occupied territory. They were a constant worry for him. Over 35 and one of the most senior members of the crew, Gonzales was efficient, devoted and remarkably talented. He could climb a coconut tree like a monkey and could sever a coconut with the skill of a practiced native. His English was limited but improved in time as he fraternized with the crew. Early in the cruise he was asked to make some lemonade. Trying to do his best he went to the galley, took five lemons and four eggs and proceeded to make "lemon-egg". I didn't sample the result but those who did said it was a gastronomic disaster.

Dominic Porta, Machinist's Mate First Class, was from Palo Alto. A happily married man, he proudly displayed pictures of his son who was born one month before we sailed. Strong as an ox, he knew his trade well. Aside from his work he was just a big playful overgrown kid and a joy to have on board.

Eugene Vossler, Electrician's Mate First Class, was from Los Angeles. He was quiet , unassuming, sensible and intelligent. He was also the oldest man on the ship and had seen action in World War I. We later promoted him to Chief. Ray Pollock, Seaman Second Class, was a young hillbilly from Arkansas. He sang songs in his Arkansas twang from morning to night, a limited but pleasant contribution to the life of the ship. A total of 15 states were represented in this diverse collection of sailors.

As a neophite I took naive comfort in the knowledge that our ship's commander was a seasoned pro with six months of prior sea duty in Alaskan waters. That was the limit of Art Bergstrom's sea-going experience, but he had the calm reassuring quality of strong leadership. A tall slim blonde of Scandinavian heritage, Art was levelheaded, fair, and open-minded. He had high principles and inspired unwavering confidence. We were fortunate to have such a man as our skipper. A native of Oregon, Art adapted well to the Navy life with admirable commitment to the ideals of the gentleman officer.

Al Farrell, the only married man of the three, was from New Orleans. Both Al and his glamorous wife, Wessie, reflected their French Cajun origins. Al had dark hair, dark eyes and matinee idol good looks. He liked jazz and with Wessie had frequented the French Quarter bistros where they could hear such greats as pianist Art Tatum. Al had no prior sea-going experience and did not fit the profile of a dedicated officer. Easy going and affable, he nevertheless fit the pattern of compatibility required for a small group of men living for extended periods in close quarters.

The ten APc's which sailed from San Pedro Harbor on March 22, 1943 would not have frightened the enemy. The four 20 mm anti-aircraft guns mounted on each ship were not obvious and a casual observer might have thought that the tuna fleet was putting out to sea. The two ships which accompanied us, a merchant tanker and a converted yacht which carried food supplies, did nothing to suggest that the tides of war were changing in our favor.

The departure was orderly and our approach to the open sea was exhilarating. If the crew was apprehensive they didn't show it. Instead there was an air of excitement and relief that at last we were getting underway. Their jovial mood soon gave way to dispair as we plunged into the stormy seas. Despite a diet of seasick pills most of them headed for the rail and spent the next few days in retching discomfort. My only problem with the rough seas was a sleepless night, clutching wildly at anything within reach to keep from rolling out of my bunk.

The sea finally calmed but not before we had what could have been a major disaster. We had been given a simple code for emergency turns to port or to starboard in case a diversion was necessary. The first night out the flotilla commander flashed the proper code as a practice maneuver. Most ships turned in the right direction but one didn't and rode up on the stern of the ship it was following. Luckily the damage was minimal and we continued on.

As we headed southwest the weather warmed and the novelty of life at sea began to pall. To save our precious water supply we took salt water showers and took advantage of an occasional rain squall to enjoy a fresh water shower on the deck. All of us did routine chores, played cribbage, listened to phonograph records and wrote letters home. Many of the crew became avid readers. We had assembled a modest but quality library prior to sailing and it proved to be the perfect antidote for tedium. After finishing an absorbing book, an 18 year old crewman with a fifth grade education confessed that it was the first book he had ever read. Averaging about eight knots (our top speed was only ten) it was a long slow trip. To liven up the journey I took on the challenge of growing a mustache. It too was a slow and frustrating process. I shaved more often to highlight the light brush which was emerging but finally resorted to a dusting of shoe polish before anyone recognized it as a mustache.

There was tension and excitement as the first dim outline of an island appeared on the horizon. After 12 days at sea the anticipation of planting our legs on good old terra firma mounted as we approached Oahu. The sun rose in a clear blue sky and the seas calmed. Despite the devastation of Pearl Harbor we were sure that a tropical paradise awaited us. Few of us had ever been to Hawaii but the movies had shaped our imagination. We rounded Coco Head and sailed past Waikaiki Beach. Watching with binoculars we were able to identify such legendary landmarks as the Royal Hawaiian Hotel with its pink facade and the stately Aloha Tower which in peace-time welcomed cruise ships to the wharf in Honolulu. The balmy air, billowy clouds and patterns of green stretching to the mountain tops held out the invitation of a languorous retreat from the world as we knew it. The view had all the elements of romance but it was an illusion. The war had intruded. The destruction wrought by Japanese bombers was clearly evident as we sailed into Pearl Harbor. We passed the burned out hulls of some of our mightiest warships and observed the feverish activity as repairs were being made to restore some of the damaged ships to active service.

Because APc's bore the designation of coastal transports we speculated that our ship might be assigned to inter-island duty within the Hawaiian Islands. Our hopes were dashed the minute we pulled alongside the dock in Pearl Harbor. Waiting for us was a Navy paint crew ready to apply its decorative skills to the entire hull. It was a non-stop priority project . Every shade of green was represented in the art work that transformed the ship from its dull grey exterior into a blend of tropical grasses. Within 24 hours the ship was completely camouflaged, an ominous signal that we were headed well beyond Hawaii to less glamorous reaches of the Pacific. To affirm this impression we were issued an enormous camouflage net with strands of green and brown cloth to spread over the top of the ship "as needed". How wrong my Uncle Dean Dickerson had been the day he spotted an APc from the San Francisco Bay Bridge. With a sense of relief he said "Well, with a ship that small they'll never send you outside the Bay." With that thought I wondered what other surprises lay ahead and turned to more immediate priorities. Throwing aside any concerns about the adventurous future that awaited us, Art Bergstrom, Al Farrell and I headed for the Officers' Club and toasted our safe arrival with more than one overdue highball.

"And What Did We See, We Saw The Sea"

It was a week of whirlwind activity in Hawaii with little time for sightseeing. From the time our ship arrived in Pearl Harbor on April 3 until it sailed again on April 9 there were stores to replenish, maintenance to be done and training for the amphibious assaults for which we were destined. Trips into Honolulu and Waikiki were infrequent, but the obligatory gas masks we had to carry, the barbed wire on the beaches, and an 8 P.M. curfew put a damper on what in normal times could have been pleasant holiday outings.

The Royal Hawaiian Hotel had been taken over by the military but the serene and regal Moana was still open to the public. With an ocean breeze blowing across its wide verandas and into the spacious dining room, the stately frame hostelry was a restful haven for weary sailors. My recollection of the hotel with its wide expanse of beach, uncluttered by the highrise buildings now crowding the water's edge, is a memorable vignette of my first visit to Waikiki.

Our crowded schedule included three days of intensive amphibious landing training off the western coast of Maui. It was there in Maalaea Bay that we tested the concept of sending troops ashore in the small inflatable rubber boats we had been issued. Propelled by noisy outboard motors, the boats were expected to carry small contingents of men in surprise assaults on an unsuspecting enemy. The first and to my knowledge the last time the plan was put into practice was during an Allied attack on the island of New Britain in 1943. None of the soldiers aboard the rubber boats survived, giving credence to skepticism expressed by some of our crew members during the Maui maneuvers. Our APc flotilla was operating in the Solomon Islands at the time and fortunately was not involved.

Meanwhile the Navy had designed and delivered the LCI (Landing Craft Infantry) with a flat bottom, steel hull, landing ramp, and protective firepower. The LCI could carry troops directly to shore, lower the ramp and provide fire cover while the men took their positions. With the development of the LCI, the APc with its rubber boats and outboard motors became obsolete and not a moment too soon. The APc's were no match for the Japanese, but the LCI's were effective and played a major role in the Allies' successful efforts to recapture the island territories overrun by the Japanese early in the war.

Pearl Harbor was a full service Navy base and it had spoiled us. All of our needs had been met with dispatch even though an APc did not carry the clout of a destroyer or battleship. We left the harbor with the knowledge that we would often have to fend for ourselves as we moved deeper into the South Pacific. Shortly before we sailed we learned that our next stop would be Pago Pago in Samoa. Having recently read Somerset Maughm's "Rain", my notions of Samoa were romantic and I looked forward to a visit, even a wartime visit, to the exotic islands of legend.

Enroute we fell easily into the routine we had learned so well in our many days at sea as we sailed to Hawaii. We were also better prepared for the rough seas which plagued us for much of the trip. I was reminded time and time again during my Navy service of the words from a popular song, "We joined the Navy to see the world, and what did we see, we saw the sea. We saw the Pacific and the Atlantic, but the Atlantic isn't romantic and the Pacific isn't what it's cracked up to be." Irving Berlin, who wrote the song, might well have added "and the Pacific isn't pacific." The song concludes: "We never get seasick sailing the ocean, we don't object to feeling the motion, we're never seasick, but we're awful sick of sea." *

Four days after we left Hawaii, I wrote:

> "Since we last got underway the sea has been so rough that it has everyone worn out. A few were seasick again and those of us who weren't are completely exhausted from having to absorb each roll of the ship with bent knees, careening stomachs and outstretched arms. I could make a fortune with the APc-37 by bringing it to the amusement park at Conneaut Lake — there are still fools who would enjoy a ride like this! Many of the men haven't been able to sleep a wink since we left. Fortunately, the rolling tends to lull me into a sound sleep. Because of the rough sea, the galley has been secured much

---

* *Irving Berlin*

of the time, and our meals have been lunches of peanut butter sandwiches, apples, pickles, etc. Tonight it is a little calmer so we had a regular meal of cold cuts, avocado salad, grape juice, peaches and pears — a meal which I topped off with a 5 cent chocolate bar from our ship's store. Our water supply and hence our baths are limited, so we all took advantage of a rain shower today for a good fresh water bath on the open deck."

The monotony of eleven days at sea was broken midway between Pearl Harbor and Pago Pago when we crossed the Equator. First-timers, and that included most of us, had to undergo initiation into "the solemn mysteries of the Ancient Order of the Deep" whereupon we became Shellbacks subject to the rule and protection of Neptunus Rex, Ruler of the Raging Main. The ceremony was reminiscent of fraternity hazing with lots of good natured bantering and highjinks.

Shellback Certificate, presented when I crossed the equator and was initiated into the Ancient Order of the Deep.

Tutuila, the main island of American Samoa, seemed to rise out of the early morning mist like a mystical fantasy. At first the dim outline of the island appeared as a purple and dark green monolith against the pale blue and golds of the morning sky. As we neared, lush greens of every shade spilled down the volcanic mountainsides and magnificent waves crashed against a rocky shore. There was no evidence of an entrance to the well defined harbor which showed on our charts. Then as we rounded a promontory there was an opening which took us into a picture postcard setting. Formed by a crater, surrounded by mountains, and almost landlocked, Pago Pago is an artist's paradise. Here and there along the shore were clusters of thatched huts and we could catch glimpses of sturdy natives with their colorful lava lavas strolling along the beach.

The village of Pago Pago was small with a concentration of frame buildings, including the U.S. colonial headquarters, lining the main street and residential cottages spreading out among the trees. There was a small Naval presence but looking across the placid bay there was virtually no suggestion of the mighty wartime struggle in which we were involved. It was one of those romantic spots, like Mikonos in the Greek Islands, where you are tempted to say "Stop the world. I want to get off." The Samoans are a proud and handsome people. As Polynesians they have light brown skin and a graceful bearing. Both men and women wear the lava lava, a bright wraparound garment that covers the body from waist to ankle. In town the women covered their breasts, but not in the country where they are less inhibited. Our crew was fascinated by the bathing ritual in which groups of women gathered on the shore at dusk for their daily ablutions. We saw no evidence of the dreaded elephantiasis disease which we heard later was decimating the Samoan population.

Rain or shine many Samoans strolled along, tall and erect, carrying umbrellas. An old man on his way to church left an indelible memory. In spite of his age he had a splendid physique, snow white hair, a clean white lava lava, and a large black umbrella. The natives took delight in saluting us. When we returned the salute they were all smiles.

As we left Samoa and headed for the Fiji Islands sceptics might have challenged the idea that we were engaged in a military operation. But our island hopping from one exotic port to another was most likely an effort to protect our vulnerable little ships from the enemy by taking a Southern route. After a five day cruise through calm seas we sailed into Suva Harbor on my 23rd birthday, April 29. Suva, the capital of the Fijis, was a decided contrast to Pago Pago.

Suva was a bustling port with cargo ships, inter-island steamers and Naval vessels crowding the harbor. It appeared to be a tropical melting pot of many nationalities. There was a sense of East meets West as we observed the British, Indians, Europeans, Chinese and other Asians mingling with the native Melanesians. The streets were busy with both pedestrian and automobile traffic, but control was enforced by tall ebony-black Melanesian policemen with thick bushy hair. They stood ramrod straight on pedestals in the middle of major intersections, fearsome and resplendent in short miniskirts and Sam Brown belts over their bare muscular chests. Big open air markets were crowded with native, Western and Asian shoppers in an array of colorful costumes and conventional dress.

One evening we went to the Grand Hotel for an elegant five course dinner served by white robed Indian waiters who padded around in bare feet. The Grand was a typical colonial building with wide verandas, ceiling fans and a spacious lobby. A steady flow of foreign guests gave it an air of mystery and intrigue. Turbans, pith helmets, straw hats and bandanas were mixed in with military uniforms of almost every Allied nation. I could imagine the spies who must have been a part of the crowd. Had we been tourists we would have lingered in Suva to explore this fascinating city, but after two days we were off to yet another South Pacific port. Our destination was Noumea, New Caledonia.

The trip to Noumea was notable for an adventure in which our clumsy little fleet of APc's tangled with a large flotilla of the Seventh Fleet engaged in Naval maneuvers. Somehow in our efforts to follow the charts and stay the course we stumbled into an awesome assembly of battleships, cruisers and destroyers intent on accomplishing their mission. We zigged and zagged to avoid them, creating confusion and disrupting their simulated battle plans. At one point we had to back our engines full speed as a high speed destroyer cut across our bow. If we had illusions about the might of our small but seaworthy ships they were shattered by the experience. Admiral Kincaid, Commander of the Seventh Fleet, may have been enraged, but perhaps he wasn't. To the ships of the Seventh Fleet the APc's may have been only an insignificant nuisance. It was embarrassing but we managed to extricate ourselves and sailed into Noumea Harbor later the same day. That night Al Farrell and I were standing at the bar of the Officers' Club when we overheard two officers next to us. One of them asked the other "What in God's name were those crazy little boats trying to do when they cut into our maneuvers?" "Another foul-up", the other replied, "Heaven help the Navy." Al and I edged away before we were drawn into the conversation.

Noumea was a major crossroads for the South Pacific war effort. It was a behind-the-lines support center for the war which was being waged against the Japanese in the islands to the North. The harbor was filled with British, Australian, New Zealand, French and U.S. Navy and Merchant Marine ships. New Caledonia was a French possession and for many years had been a French penal colony. Many of Noumea's residents are descendents of French prisoners. The language is French and the city has a decidedly French flavor. In pre-war days it was referred to as the Paris of the South Pacific and was a favorite vacation spot for Australians and New Zealanders who came to enjoy the balmy climate, the French cuisine and shops filled with Parisian fashions and perfumes. World War II had transformed the city. The climate was still balmy and the countryside looked like the California coast but there was little to suggest Paris to the visiting GI. There may have been a few French bistros tucked away on the side streets, but we didn't find them. The city was overrun by servicemen and the native population didn't exactly throw out the welcome mat.

There were compensations. The Navy provided outstanding recreation programs. There were parks and beaches, basketball and volleyball courts and outdoor barbecue parties. While we were there Artie Shaw and his All Star Navy Band put on a concert for service personnel at a park in the center of town. As leader of one of the most popular "Big Bands" in America, Shaw had given up civilian life to accept an appointment as a Chief Petty Officer in the Navy. His music drew record crowds of service men and women wherever he performed.

There was also recreation of a different kind, provided not by the Navy but by a thriving enterprise famous throughout the Navy and dubbed The Pink House. Day and night there were long lines of eager sailors waiting to pay for a brief encounter, limited to 15 minutes, with one of the young or not so young ladies inside.

Although we didn't get to sample the French cuisine, we did enjoy the freshly baked bread. Not far from the ship was a bakery where crusty French bread was baked in large brick ovens right along the street. We took up a collection and each morning picked up our daily supply of bread for the entire crew. Some of us also enjoyed the luxury of clothes washed in a French laundry. Having heard of a home where laundry was done, I ventured forth with a full laundry bag only to find that no one there spoke English. In my fractured French I blurted out "Je veux se laver" which means I want a bath. By waving the laundry bag I convinced them that I wanted the clothes washed.

My wings were tested shortly before we left Noumea. We had sailed out through the harbor entrance to calibrate some equipment and were in the middle of a test run when a motor launch pulled alongside. There was an emergency meeting which called for the presence of both Art Bergstrom, our Commanding Officer, and Al Farrell, the Executive Officer. As they sped off to the meeting it dawned on me that I was the lone officer on board and for the first time completely in charge of the ship. Although I had received my promotion to Lt. (jg) on arrival in Noumea, the extra stripe on my sleeve meant little when it came to maneuvering our ship through the crowded harbor. Fortunately there were no mishaps and I managed to slide into the dock for a perfect landing. There was a cheer from the crew. I'm not sure whether it was admiration for my skill in handling the ship or relief from the terror they may have felt in having a neophyte at the helm.

Two days later, after seventeen days of preparation in Noumea, we maneuvered gingerly through poorly marked mine fields just outside the harbor to embark on the final leg of our journey into the South Pacific battle zone.

Iron Bottom Bay

As we sailed out of Noumea Harbor there was a sense that we were leaving behind the last semblance of civilization. To the North there were the islands of Melanesia, peopled by primitive negroid tribes and largely bypassed by the twentieth century until the Japanese made them a battleground in World War II. On their march to extend Japanese influence throughout Southeast Asia the Japanese had occupied many of the islands and were stopped only when U.S. forces took a stand in the Solomon Islands. It was the day before we left Noumea that we learned for sure that our final destination was Guadalcanal in the Solomons. Guadalcanal had already been secured by Allied troops and aircraft but there were still pockets of guerrilla resistance and daily attacks by Japanese bombers and fighter planes.

The trip north from New Caledonia had many of the elements of a South Seas vacation cruise. The waters were clear and calm. Flying fish winged out of the sea and occasionally landed on our decks. At night the constellations were clear and brilliant with the Southern Cross dramatically etched in the sky. Gliding along, with the water lapping gently against the hull, the porpoises would come to play. Leaping in and out of the water on both sides of the bow they seemed to be in a joyous race with the ship. They left a glowing trail of luminescence in the water. In the quiet of the midnight watch, with the ship darkened and only a skeleton crew on duty, it was refreshing to stand on the flying bridge, cooled by the balmy breezes, and watch for distant islands which were often silhouetted in the moonlight. During the day we trolled for fish with a rig which the crew had fashioned and one day caught a 40 pound tuna. It was enough for the entire crew and a nice change from our diet of Spam and other canned meats.

Half way to the Solomons we made a brief stop at Espiritu Santo, a flat palm covered island in the New Hebrides chain. It was the locale of the postwar musical South Pacific starring Mary Martin and Ezio Pinza and from a distance the waving palms suggested a South Seas paradise. On shore the reality of war was evident with military vehicles crowding makeshift roads, docks loaded with military supplies and the roar of aircraft taking off on training missions. After refueling and taking on supplies we sailed on to Guadalcanal while the weather became more steamy and oppressive. We didn't need a map to tell us that Guadalcanal is just ten degrees south of the equator. Unlike many of the other islands in the area it is mountainous with lush green peaks rising dramatically from the sea to over 8000 feet. We headed for the harbor at Lunga and saw an inviting sandy beach stretching for several miles. While we waited for orders from the local amphibious command, most of the crew headed for the beach for a welcome swim after the long hot voyage.

It was then that we began to understand the meaning of that celebrated Navy phrase, SNAFU, Situation Normal All Fouled Up. The command to which we had orders to report had never heard of the U.S.S. APc-37 and its sister ships. Suddenly we were a ship without a country and it took two or three days before they received the communication which gave them the authority to accept us. Meanwhile we anchored offshore and scrounged for the supplies we needed to keep us in the manner to which we had become accustomed. This took some creative footwork as we finagled such important items as beer and canned chicken from Army supply depots. We stayed clear of the Navy until our arrival became official.

Once our indeterminate status was clarified we were given a permanent berthing assignment near the mouth of Hutchinson's Creek which emptied into the harbor at Tulagi on Florida Island, across a narrow strait from Guadalcanal. We tied up to a dock which supplied fresh water to small ships in the area and that was our operating base for some time to come. It soon became apparent that the role of the APc's was to haul supplies and sometimes troops to nearby island bases. By the time we arrived in Guadalcanal the flat bottomed LCI (Landing Craft Infantry) had displaced the APc as a more suitable vessel for amphibious assaults. We were therefore relegated to serve as an inter-island shipping and transportation service.

When we arrived in late May 1943, Japanese ground troops had already surrendered on Guadalcanal, but the air war over the Solomons was still in progress. In early June the Japanese made one last desperate attempt to show their air superiority and sent squadrons of bombers and fighter planes in a major show of force. It was a daytime raid and provided a breathtaking spectacle for those of us who watched from the relative safety of our small ship. Dog fights and bursts of anti-aircraft fire could be seen in every direction. The Japanese were no match for the P-38s and other fighters of the U.S. Air Force and the U.S. victory was decisive. It was a turning point in the air war and from then on Japanese air raids in the Guadalcanal sector were limited to nightly bombing attacks which were largely ineffective.

MTB Squadron 9, a squadron of twelve PT boats, was based across the inlet, a short distance from our berth. When they needed fresh water they would tie alongside our ship and stretch the hoses across our deck to fill their tanks. Shortly after we settled in at Tulagi I was doing some paper work in the wardroom of our ship when I heard Art Bergstrom say "And this is the wardroom" to a visitor he was showing around. The visitor looked in and I did a double take. It was my good friend, classmate, and Phi Delt fraternity brother from Allegheny College, Dave Robertson. I couldn't believe my eyes and neither could he. He was the skipper of one of the neighboring PT boats. From then on Dave and I saw alot of each other. Aside from the camaraderie, our getting together had many mutual benefits.

Limited as the facilities were on our ship, they were better than Dave had on shore in his Spartan camp of tents and tropical insects. In his spare time Dave came often to the ship to enjoy a good meal, take a shower, iron his clothes, and play poker with us til the wee hours. He liked our cuisine and for good reason. Curtin was a creative cook and did wonders with a limited range of menu possibilities. He also had the advantage of a well stocked freezer which we replenished from the reefer ships at every opportunity. After dining on filet mignon one night Dave said he had been to the Mark Hopkins, the Biltmore, and the Waldorf-Astoria but had never had a steak as good as the one he was served on the APc-37. The distance from those culinary havens of gourmet cooking may possibly have affected his judgement, and mine as well, but none of us suffered from a starvation diet. What we missed most were the fresh foods like lettuce, assorted vegetables, eggs, ice cream, and milk. Dehydrated milk, eggs, and potatoes were not good substitutes.

Money was useless in the Solomons but the barter system flourished. One day I traded a 70 pound sack of sugar with Dave Robertson for a two gallon drum of hard candy. Natives from nearby villages would come by in dugout canoes with stalks of fresh bananas, pineapples, wood carvings, and trinkets made from bone and shells. For these we traded cigarettes, pipes, candy, and articles of clothing. They particularly valued undershorts or "skivvies" as we called them.

Although Dave liked to come to our ship, we liked to visit the PT base because they had movies. We would crank up the outboard motor on our skiff and travel for about ten minutes across the inlet to the base. One night the movie was interrupted by an air raid. We decided we should try to get back to the ship, but we couldn't get the outboard started. Fortunately we had oars and with shrapnel falling all around us we rowed almost as fast as if the outboard were working. It was a relief to hear the "all clear" signal shortly after we got to the relative safety of the ship.

There were no professional barbers among the crew but we had several volunteers who were willing to cut hair for a little extra change. The Chief Motor Machinist's Mate was reasonably expert with the clippers and after awhile I felt I could also trust our Radioman First Class to do a good job. In those days there were few beards but mustaches were fashionable. Dave had a thick bartender mustache and later traded it in for a distinguished goatee. Art Bergstrom's mustache was trim and blonde, adding just a little age to his youthful appearance. Al Farrell looked dapper with a dark mustache but mine had been a disaster and I didn't try it again.

There were long periods of leisure time between our inter-island runs. There were always maintenance and supply chores to occupy some of the time, but there was also time for socializing. Some of this took place at our favorite watering hole, The Iron Bottom Bay club on the other side of Tulagi Harbor. The club got its name from the many ships which had been lost in the battle for Guadalcanal. It was a well equipped Navy Officers' recreation center and well stocked with the finest brands of booze. In establishing new bases the officers' clubs were high on the list of Navy priorities, next to other critical facilities like air strips. On occasion we visited other ships just to get acquainted. One evening we spent aboard a New Zealand frigate drinking rum with the officers and talking about cultural differences. We noted that rum was de rigueur aboard British ships while verboten on ours. "What is this drink, Coca Cola," asked one of the officers, "and why does it have such a hold on the American people?" That was before Coca Cola had become a universal beverage of choice around the world. Today the question would never be asked.

In contrast to our elbow-bending activity we also went to church. At sea Art Bergstrom conducted simple and dignified services on Sunday mornings. In Tulagi Al Farrell rounded up the Catholics in the crew and went ashore for the 6:30 A.M. mass. Art Bergstrom and I followed with the Protestants at the more civilized hour of 9:00 A.M. The chaplain who conducted our services was dull, but the church was a knockout, constructed entirely of bamboo and palm leaves. The services improved when a portable organ was delivered from the States, courtesy of the Presbyterian Church.

Letters from home were exciting moments in the life of every sailor. After we settled into a routine at Tulagi, letters and sometimes packages arrived more frequently. There was always a clamor to greet the mail clerk when he returned from the post office. Sometimes he returned empty-handed and then we played the recording, "No Letter Today, Dear" over the loud speaker system. When letters did arrive they were read and reread. Excerpts and snapshots of wives, children, and girlfriends were often shared with other members of the crew. I received a constant flow of mail not only from the family but from many friends of all ages, some of whom I knew only casually. The correspondence reflected the strong support for servicemen during the war and kept us in touch with the home front. From time to time gifts and correspondence arrived from the many volunteer organizations which had grown up around the United States. In my home town of Meadville an organization called the Victory Volunteers published a news letter and sent gifts to servicemen throughout the year. We had subscribed to Life, Colliers, Time, The Saturday Post, and Readers Digest before we left the States. The first copies arrived a week after we hit the Solomons, a month or so out of date but welcome nevertheless. The Meadville Tribune which usually came in bunches, also out of date, kept me abreast of hometown news.

One day several crew members captured a red parrot in the nearby jungle and brought it aboard to be our mascot. They built a cage which had to be rebuilt after the independent bird chewed its way out of the first one. Then they tried to teach it how to talk. Never was a bird pampered and cajoled by more people, but it still refused to talk. After a few days it died, never having said a word. It could have been a suicide to escape from the oppression of its captors, but more likely it was the diet. The crew fed it everything from pancakes to soda crackers.

The days in port passed more slowly than those at sea but there were always chores to perform. I spent an entire morning chasing down a fresh supply of attabrine tablets which we all took daily to ward off malaria. We also took salt tablets regularly because we lost so much salt through perspiration. There was always paperwork for the officers to do. Even though we were a small ship we had to fill out the same forms required of destroyers or cruisers. It was just that our numbers were smaller. As the gunnery officer for the ship I had to make sure that the guns were in working order and adequate ammunition was on board and safely stored. I learned to clean my own gun, a .45 calibre pistol. The first time I tried, I put it back together and there was one part left over. I made sure that our experienced gunner's mate never found out. We rotated the duty officer responsibility while in port. When we had the duty we had to remain on the ship as the officer in charge. That didn't mean that we couldn't join in a game of hearts, monopoly or poker when things were quiet.

One day Dave Robertson treated me to a thrilling ride on his boat, PT-158. The PT was an 80 foot motor torpedo boat powered by three Packard engines which could cruise at speeds up to 35 knots. It was a practice run but Dave put the boat through its paces. The bow rose out of the water as we cut through the waves at breakneck speeds. When you ride on a PT you have to hang on. It was like a bucking bronco. It was exhilarating to feel the power of the engines and the ocean spray washing across our faces. It was a different experience by far from the ride on our slow moving APc.

One morning a jubilant Dave Robertson told us that his boat with others in his squadron had torpedoed a Japanese cruiser in Blackett Strait off the coast of Kolombangara Island. They had been engaged in operations the night before in an area just north of New Georgia. Later in the day word began to filter back that an American ship, the U.S.S. McCawley, had been sunk in the same spot. There was an embarrassing silence at the PT base until Dave quietly suggested that we forget the good news of the morning. His squadron had in fact sunk the McCawley. It was one of those classic examples of poor communications. The McCawley, a former P & O liner converted to an amphibious transport, had been evacuated after a fire and was being towed through enemy waters to a safe harbor. The attack squadron of PT boats had not been notified of the movement. When the darkened ship failed to respond to a signal code challenge, the

PTs launched torpedoes. It didn't help to learn that the McCawley was serving as the flagship for Admiral Richmond Kelly Turner, Commander Amphibious Forces South Pacific.

From time to time there were little vignettes of local color which made the war seem more distant. One evening at sunset I looked out from the bridge of our ship and saw two dugout canoes filled with natives paddling in synchronized rhythm. As the natives sang a haunting song, the boats glided gracefully through the water until they disappeared and the voices were just an echo. It was a scene I shall never forget.

Beer was the only alcoholic beverage Navy ships were permitted to carry but it had to be consumed on shore. It was a rare but welcome treat in the hot climate and from time to time we were issued a few cases. We had been without beer for a long period when we noticed several of the crew staggering around the deck in a calm sea. We began looking for booze and discovered that one of our ingenious engineers had converted our trusty washing machine into a still. We had to admire his creativity but Navy discipline prevailed. The washing machine was a treasure. It was not standard equipment for an APc and I wondered what the Navy had in mind by not providing one. Cleanliness is next to Godliness in the Navy and we did not want to rely on shore based installations for laundry service. While our ship was being equipped and provisioned at the shipyard in San Francisco I had gone to the government Priorities Board to get a priority for purchasing a washing machine. They said "yes, if you can find one." Newly manufactured washing machines were simply not available because the factories that made them had been converted to the production of military hardware. The Priorities Board went to bat for us and after a dozen phone calls located a second hand Thor. We had it reconditioned until it was as good as new, not realizing how versatile it might become.

Also non-standard was the bicycle we acquired. We thought that it might come in handy when we were in port. The red tape we went through to get it was unbelievable. First I went to the regional director of the Office of Price Administration to get authorization to purchase a bicycle. The regional director called the state director and the state director called the local director. After a series of telephone calls we received a letter authorizing a bicycle for the ship. Then I had to take the letter to the Rationing Board. The Rationing Board called a meeting of its members who deliberated and finally gave us permission to make the purchase. One of the Board members asked if we planned to put pontoons on the bicycle. He had a point. It turned out that we seldom used it. There were few docks in the Solomons and we usually anchored. We finally sold the bike to a shore based unit for $60. We had paid $40 in San Francisco.

One of my favorite pastimes was reading. Our library was well stocked for such a small ship and new books kept arriving as gifts from family and friends. On our extended trip across the Pacific I read such books as "Green Light", a novel by Lloyd Douglas, "The Trembling Of A Leaf" by Somerset Maughm, "Extracts From 'History' by Herodotus", "Through The Alimentary Canal With Gun and Camera", "Murder Day By Day" by Irvin S. Cobb, and a story about the eskimos, "Kabloona", which helped me to "think cool" as we headed into a warmer climate. Thanks to a Navy Chaplain who gave me a copy of "The New Testament", I finally got around to reading that fascinating account of the Christian story from start to finish. After we based in Tulagi I read "The Late George Apley", a wonderful story with a Boston setting (George Arless starred in the movie version) and a novel by Paul Gallico, "Keeping Cool At Conneaut" which painted a sordid picture of Conneaut Lake Park, a popular resort near my home town of Meadville.

Solomons Mop-Up

The nightly air raids we experienced at Tulagi were more of a nuisance than a threat. Japanese air power had been severely crippled in the big air battle we witnessed in early June. Ground positions on Guadalcanal and Tulagi had been well established and the Allies were on the offensive to recapture the remaining Solomons. Air strips had been built on the Russell Islands a short distance northwest of Guadalcanal as a base for the attack on New Georgia, the next major island in the chain. The Japanese were well entrenched at Munda on New Georgia but the Allies had established a beachhead on nearby Rendova Island. It was about that time in late June of 1943 that our base was shifted to the north from Tulagi to Pavuvu, the largest island of the Russell group.

The Russells had been the site of a large coconut plantation with a flat expanse of waving palms edged with sandy beaches. Today those islands would be a prime location for a resort hotel. We were given docking space at a wooden pier near the end of the landing strip. It was convenient for the services we needed but hazardous when the Japanese planes decided to bomb the air strip. One night in particular Japanese dive bombers made successive runs at the air strip, frequently missing their prime target and narrowly missing our ship. Bombs were dropping to the right and left of us and shrapnel from anti-aircraft fire was raining down on the ship. Our helmets withstood the shower of shrapnel but we had some tense moments.

While the battle for New Georgia raged, the APc-37 and several of its sister ships made frequent runs to carry supplies and troops to Rendova, the Allied island base across a narrow strait from Japanese held Munda. Rendova had a good, almost landlocked harbor, with a coral reef at the entrance. Only shallow draft vessels were able to enter and even they could enter only at high tide. On our first visit we carefully approached the entrance and cringed as we heard and felt the ship scraping across the reef. It was on that visit that we went ashore, with guns from Allied emplacements thundering away at the Japanese across the strait. After conducting our business we were ushered to a tent where a rumpled group of Army officers were having the equivalent of a mid-morning coffee break. They gave us tin canteen cups and shared their supply of canned grapefruit juice and "torpedo juice", the alcohol used in torpedo tubes. One sip and your entire digestive tract is on fire.

The farther we moved from the major supply base at Guadalcanal the more we had to use our ingenuity to stretch the supplies that we had. When we ran out of fresh meat we went fishing for shark, always plentiful in the island waters and big enough to feed the entire crew. One day we caught four barracuda, one of which was 3 feet 7 inches long. In the hands of our competent cook, barracuda became a favorite seafood delicacy. Better yet was the freshly caught tuna. Our prize catch was a 90 pound tuna which must have been something of a record. It was five feet long and 34 inches around the middle.

In our new advanced base location, mail deliveries became more sporadic and morale sometimes suffered. At one point we went two months without pay. With nothing much to buy, that wasn't a great inconvenience except to serious poker enthusiasts. Beautiful scenery and the company of the same people, and all men at that, weren't enough to offset the boredom that often set in. Ashore there were no stores, no paved streets, no women, and no automobiles — only jeeps and Army trucks causing traffic jams on crushed coral roads. In that atmosphere our operational runs and the occasional excitement created by Japanese aircraft or snipers were a welcome break in the routine.

Eugene E. Vossler, CEM and John Wm. Hereford, QM1/C proudly displaying their 90 lb. tuna catch.

As they moved up through the islands, the Allies were successful in routing most of the Japanese. Some they deliberately bypassed and some managed to escape into the jungle where they used guerrilla tactics to harass American personnel. For the most part they were just a nuisance and were gradually cleaned out, but they could be deadly. An officer from one of our sister APc's was returning to his ship in an outboard motor boat when rifle shots rang out. Two crew members who were with him ducked down as the bullets whizzed by. Thinking that some Americans were carelessly shooting in his direction, he stood up and hollered for them to stop. He was an easy target and became the first victim of Japanese snipers that I knew personally. Just the night before he had been aboard our ship playing poker and proudly showing snapshots of his wife and infant boy.

Despite the oppressive heat during the day those of us on Navy ships had some relief in the evening when it cooled off and there were faint breezes blowing across the water. Our shore based friends weren't so lucky. They suffered from the heat and humidity. They also had to cope with insects, particularly mosquitoes. At night when we went ashore for movies, we donned long sleeve shirts and trousers, liberally applying insect repellant and hoping that the outdoor theater area had been freshly sprayed. Aboard ship we dressed for hot weather which usually meant khaki shorts and no shirt. Ashore we switched to the prevailing dress code for officers: long khaki trousers, khaki shirt with no tie, overseas cap, and jungle shoes. The official dress whites intended for the tropics were never worn in the Solomons. As a stunt I appeared in my dress whites one afternoon and the crew thought I was an apparition.

Rats were another problem. We were successful for a long time in keeping them off the ship, but one hot night when I was sleeping in the buff I woke up with a start to discover a rat scampering down my chest. We got rid of the rats but made friends with the cockroaches on the theory that if you can't lick 'em, join 'em.

Throughout my Navy experience I continued to run across good friends from Meadville and Allegheny. Dick Jones, a Phi Gam who graduated a year ahead of me at Allegheny, managed a large supply operation in the Russells. We saw a great deal of each other and he was helpful in guiding me through the red tape of requisitioning supplies. We became well acquainted with the Naval supply system and learned that Supply Officers could have a sense of humor. At a Navy warehouse I had inadvertantly filled in a requisition for 'five gallons of swabs'. The Supply Officer looked at me curiously, then laughed and said "Everyone gets that way when they have been out here long enough." "Pretty soon we're going to start issuing paint by the bushel."

On another junket to pick up supplies I took along some of the crew and borrowed a truck from a motor pool. The truck was in bad shape

with its top torn off, no brakes, and six different shifts which func-
tioned erratically. All the men piled inside except for one who rode
on the hood as a lookout. I made the mistake of assuming the gear
shift was the same as the family Buick. As a result we almost
plunged through the parking lot fence instead of backing out of the
entrance as I intended. I also forgot to notice that the gas gauge was
almost on empty and we barely made it to a gas station on appropriately named Russell Boulevard. I had one of the men posted on the
emergency brake which served the purpose but brought us to sudden and jerky stops which almost sent everyone through the wind-
shield. Having stocked up on necessities I decided to try my luck for
an ice cream freezer. For months I had been trying to find one but
had been told each time that they were not available. This time when
I posed the question the Supply Officer replied "I don't see why not".
We were jubilant. Another unexpected treat that day was Coca Cola
which we began to think had not made its way beyond Pearl Harbor.
I found it by stumbling into the wrong warehouse where it was
stored. Another trip back to the Supply Officer and we were the
proud owners of five cases.

Dave Robertson surfaced from time to time between runs into enemy
territory. The base for his PT boat squadron had also been shifted to
the Russells. We welcomed his visits, not only for the camaraderie,
but because we knew that the galley staff would stir up an excep-
tional meal for the occasion. Dave was popular with all on board. We
were disappointed when we learned that he had been transferred
back to the States for medical treatment of a serious eye infection.

Munda finally fell to the Allies on August 4, 1943. The following
week Boyce Dunnigan and I paid a visit to the home of Captain
Donald C. Kennedy, a coastwatcher on New Georgia who had operated a clandestine short wave radio behind the Japanese lines. (Boyce
was a fellow APc officer and former Meadville High School student
of my vintage.) Captain Kennedy was one of a number of fearless
and dashing Australian patriots who remained in the Solomons after
the Japanese invasion to feed information to the Allied command.
Many of them had been administrators or plantation managers who
were given commissions by the Australian Navy. Captain Kennedy's
exploits were legend. He had mustered a small army of natives to
serve as an armed guard as he shifted his location from time to time
to deceive the Japanese who had a price on his head. He also had a

small armada of schooners that he used to harass the Japanese and rescue both American and Japanese pilots. Arriving at Captain Kennedy's compound we were met by one of his armed guards, a jet black Melanesian, wearing a breech clout and a red hibiscus blossom in his hair.

We walked up a long driveway lined with yellow, red, and orange hibiscus and at the top of a rise came to a large frame house with a wide veranda stretching around the front and sides. It was a peaceful setting which belied the conflict which had been raging in the area. The colorful Captain was a gracious host. He served us tea on the veranda and kept us spellbound for two hours with tales of his adventures. Our visit took on special significance when he told us that he had received a radio message that morning from a nearby coastwatcher with the news that Jack Kennedy and ten other survivors had been rescued several days after their PT boat was cut in two by a Japanese destroyer in the waters off New Georgia. Operating as one of the PT boats in Dave Robertson's squadron, Kennedy's boat had separated from the others in a major skirmish and was run down by a destroyer trying to escape from Allied ships that were in pursuit. That story is documented in the book "PT 109" by Robert J. Donovan.

The Allies moved north and west in their successful campaign to recapture the Solomons occupied by the Japanese. After securing New Georgia, the next stop was Bougainville. In case we had settled in to enjoy the relative peace and tranquility of our inter-island transport service, a message we received in the fall of 1943 was designed to get our adrenalin flowing. The message carried orders for us to proceed to Treasury Island just off the south coast of Bougainville on D Minus 5 Day! It startled us out of any lethargy we may have been experiencing. The APc-37 was to be part of an advance task force to establish a base from which Allied planes and ships could carry on the campaign to invade Bougainville. A key element in the strategy was the immediate construction of an airstrip by the Navy Seabees. The Seabees were the unsung heroes of World War II. Their motto was 'The difficult we do today; the impossible takes a little longer.' Their performance attested to the validity of the motto.

Travelling at night, shrouded by a camouflage net from stem to stern, we arrived at dawn off the coast of Treasury Island. The island had been undergoing heavy bombardment from Navy cruisers. Allied planes were bombing selective targets and providing air cover for the ships. Insignificant as they may have seemed, the APc's were playing a key role, carrying troops and drums of high test ethyl gasoline. As we approached the harbor we heard a frantic message from the Allied Command asking which of our ships was firing anti-aircraft guns at friendly planes. The culprit turned out to be one of our sister APc's, skippered by a notoriously inept former school teacher. In his embarassment he came too close to shore and sheered off the limbs of a tree which had tangled with the mast. He quickly reversed direction and as we entered the harbor he was leaving.

We proceeded to the center of the harbor, and without dropping anchor, began to unload both troops and cargo. Meanwhile, Japanese gun batteries were lobbing shells into several LCI's and LST's which had lowered their ramps on the beach to unload both supplies and troops. Apparently they were more attractive targets, because we were left alone. A few Japanese planes managed to get through the Allied air cover and added to the excitement. One Japanese Zero skimmed across the water so close to our ship that we could see the determined expression on the face of the pilot. Our anti-aircraft guns opened fire but reacted too slowly to be effective. In disgust, Curtin the cook said "I could have hit him with a potato."

Toward evening, mission accomplished, the "37" headed out to sea in company with one of the LST's. We moved at a snail's pace because neither of the ships was known for speed. We used to say that LST stood for "Large Stationary Target". Shortly before midnight we were spotted by a Japanese reconnaisance plane which dropped flares and then bombs. In our vulnerability we pursued a zig-zag course, a strategy which worked. Having dropped what may have been its only bombs, the plane turned and left. It had been a tense moment.

During the late fall and into the winter of 1943 we continued to ply the reef laden waters of the Solomons as a combination truck and bussing service for the troops. We referred to it as "yard bird" duty or the "milk run". At one point I contracted a fever which threw me into the hospital on Pavuvu. I was running a temperature of 104 and was so weak I could scarcely move. At my weakest moment there was a Japanese air raid and we had to crawl out of our hospital cots and into foxholes until the all clear was given. The hospital was a Quonset hut with screened-in sides but the doctoring and nursing care was excellent. I was out and feeling fine within a week.

There was a feeling of fraternal collegiality among most of the officers in our APc flotilla. Some of us had been together at Midshipmen's School and we had shared the experience of sailing across a vast expanse of the Pacific to the Solomon Islands war zone. An exception was an arrogant young martinet who commanded one of the little APc's as though it were a battleship. He had delusions of grandeur about the role of the "captain" and isolated himself from the other two officers and his crew. When he roped off a large section of the deck and designated it "officers' country" the crew was ready to mutiny. Only 'he' could give orders to the engine room and the deck hands as the ship was approaching or leaving the dock. That led to some problems. The biggest problem was that he was inept. Once when his ship was landing at a finger pier, he inadvertently gave orders to the engine room to go ahead full speed instead of reverse. The engine room, which had often been on the receiving end of his vituperative criticism, followed his orders to the letter. They revved up the engines to full speed, the ship shuddered and plunged onto the beach where it came to a jolting stop. Another time he gave the order to cast off the lines as the ship was leaving the dock, but he forgot the bow line. The ship lurched and swung around as the junior officers and crew stood in amused silence. The Filipino steward bore much of the brunt of the captain's abusive behavior. Proud and hot-headed, he confided to one of the junior officers that he planned to kill the captain. It seemed to be more than just an idle threat, so we arranged to transfer him to our ship, the APc-37, in exchange for Gonzales, our able and hopefully more level headed steward. The Navy brass finally got wise to this personification of Captain Queeg and transferred him to shore duty in the States.

In another incident, perhaps apocryphal but well communicated through the APc grapevine, a lookout spotted a torpedo heading straight for his ship. He reported it to the bridge where the skipper was standing watch. In a panic the skipper jumped overboard without issuing orders to abandon ship. The torpedo struck the side of the ship and pierced two bulkheads before lodging in the engine room. The crew remained on board but fished the skipper out of the water when it became apparent the torpedo was a dud. That was a rare case of reprehensible behavior. The great majority of the young officers with whom I came in contact exercised remarkable maturity and judgement. Considering their youth and inexperience they performed with a competence which was a credit to the Navy's selection and training system.

In late December Art Bergstrom received orders transferring him back to the States. Jim Gott was transferred from another APc to take his place. Within a few weeks I was promoted to the position of Executive Officer on the U.S.S. APc-29. I stayed aboard the "37" through Christmas and moved to the new ship on December 29, 1943. Our South Sea Island Christmas took place in the middle of the Solomon Islands summer. The sun was warm, the palms rustled in the breeze, parrots and exotic butterflies circled the ship and natives paddled by in small canoes. It was a far cry from a white Christmas, but another APc with a Marine band and a group of carolers sailed slowly around the harbor to give us a nostalgic touch of the Christmases we had known.

The Captain of the "29" was Charles O. Bower, my former roommate during Midshipmen's training at Northwestern University in Chicago. We got along well together and teamed up for a new phase of activity in the Northern Solomons.

The Mosquito Network

It was easy to adjust to the APc - 29. The ship was a twin of the "37." The skipper, Chuck Bower, and I were already good friends. Chuck was a 29 year old accountant from Chicago's North Side and a graduate of Grinnell Colllege in Iowa. Both the "37" and the "29" had made the long journey across the Pacific together and the operational assignments were similar. With only three officers, one had to be a jack-of-all trades on an APc, so my duties were largely unchanged. Personnel is a major responsibility of the Executive Officer. He handles much of the administration which means more reports and as a backup to the Captain he is involved in more ship handling, a job that I relished.

The "29" had a top notch crew, but I had been spoiled on the APc-37. Before I left, our Ship's Cook, Curtin, said "Mr. Schultz, when you get aboard the "29" you'll find out how much I spoiled you" and he was right. Stokes, the cook on the "29" was no match for Curtin but he knew how to bake, and apple pies were his specialty. Fortunately Stokes had more to work with. By the time of my transfer we were getting more fresh foods. There was a fairly steady supply of meats, potatoes, onions, cabbage, cauliflour, and butter and occasionally there were oranges, pears and apples. Eggs and milk were still non-existent except in powdered form. Everything else came from cans.

The Steward's Mate on the "29" was named Tolliver, a 19 year old black from Houston. Again, we had been spoiled on the APc-37 with the spit and polish service of Gonzales. The Navy expected its officers to be catered to as gentlemen, even on little wash tubs like ours in the far reaches of the Pacific. Gonzales was a pro and a hard act to follow. But Tolliver cheerfully tried and in time measured up to his predecessor. Unfortunately blacks and other minorities were relegated in those days to such jobs as Steward's Mate. Tolliver had the potential for more challenging responsibilities and was proud of the fact that his father worked for the Southern Pacific Railroad. By late spring Tolliver had mastered the job. The silver was polished, the wardroom was spotless and he was a model waiter.

Haggling with the natives had become something of a sport which both parties enjoyed. As the war continued the natives had fine-tuned the negotiating process. One day two of them approached me with a beautiful ebony cane. Hand carved, it was shaped at the top like a crouching cat. The cat with mother of pearl eyes was peering into the eyes of a snake which curled up from the bottom. "A fine ebony cane", said one. "Usually sells for $16." Then to soften me up "We help Americans fight Japs." Back and forth, back and forth, until we finally settled for two cans of biscuits. At one point they offered me $5 for one can of biscuits. They wanted biscuits. I wanted the cane. Everyone was happy.

Rough seas usually meant a rough trip, even for those of us who did-n't get seasick. We could start out in a calm sea with sunny skies and with virtually no warning be enveloped in a fierce tropical squall. The waves could reach almost typhoon proportions. On one such occasion we sought overnight shelter in a rockbound cove and spent an all night vigil trying to keep our anchor from dragging. In another incident we left port one morning at dawn and ran headlong into the face of a brewing storm. Because they had had night watch-es, Chuck Bower and Floyd Eckert, the third officer, slept in while I took over the conn and headed out to sea. In no time we were plung-ing through mountainous waves. I donned foul weather gear and hung on to the guard rail while we rose on the crest of a wave and plunged almost vertically down the other side. The elements seemed to be having a wild and glorious time, so I joined in with song. Singing at the top of my lungs I covered a repertoire from Bach to Mamie Reilly. It was an exhilarating experience. When confronted with seas of that magnitude I often wondered how Christopher Columbus was able to cope in a ship even smaller than ours. His flagship, the Santa Maria, was the largest of his fleet and yet was only 90 feet long.

While based at the island of Rendova we arranged for a large motor launch to take us on a hunting and fishing expedition. I joined those of the crew who were interested and we pulled away from the ship in a jumble of rifles, pistols, fishing tackle, sandwiches, raincoats, and water canteens. The latter may have been the most important because the hot sun dehydrated us in a hurry. No sooner had we cleared the harbor than one of the men had his first strike, a medi-um sized barracuda. From then on it was one fish after another as the boat idled slowly over coral reefs between nearby islands. There were mackerel, bonitos, red snapper, tuna, king fish and several that we couldn't identify.

Finally we approached a small uninhabited island surrounded by coral and lava reefs. Landing by motor launch was impossible, so the five of us who wanted to go hunting jumped into the surf in water up to our chests. Commando style we waded and plunged ahead, a difficult ordeal because we were walking over the knife sharp edges of the coral. After several hundred yards we reached the beach and prepared for our push into the jungle. The island we had chosen was known locally as an ideal hunting area for doves, but to get to them we had to penetrate into the deepest part of the jungle. It was my first taste of a real jungle, untouched by man. Tall trees with a heavy growth of dark green leaves served as columns to support the inter-woven mat of tough vines which hung overhead and shut out the rays of the sun. The ground was damp and soggy and covered with the decay of the jungle. The underbrush was a tangle of vines and tropical plants, so thick that we had to crawl and disentangle ourselves with each step.

The mosquitos encircled us in clouds but we forged ahead. The quarry was worth the discomfort. Finally we reached an area where the doves were nesting. They were difficult to see in the grey green patterns of the trees, but I had the good fortune to bag three doves with my first three shots. I fired at a fourth but missed. Chief Petty Officer John Sanders also downed three but we couldn't locate the third after it fell. The five doves were turned into a tasty meal after we returned to the ship. On the return trip the good luck of the fishermen continued with the most exciting catch of the day, a large shark. It was landed by Weeks, a Seaman Second Class who in civilian life had been a fishing guide in Florida.

One quiet day Chuck Bower and I hired a native pilot to take us into a remote area of New Georgia to visit several native villages. The villages close to the naval bases were almost deserted as the natives removed their women and children to the relative safety of outlying islands. Many of the men remained as laborers but we had little opportunity to observe the indigenous culture. Our boat trip took us through narrow passages and lush green island foliage to a village which had been developed many years ago by British missionaries.

We had come prepared with tobacco, pipes, cigarettes, jewelry, canned salmon and canned corned beef to trade for souvenirs. The tobacco products turned out to be useless because the natives were Seventh Day Adventists. They didn't smoke!

Floyd Eckert had asked us to get him a grass skirt. When I asked one of the natives if he had any, he turned and spoke to a girl in the native tongue. She disappeared and returned with a yellow and white grass skirt. I offered a red necklace for it, but the nasty face she made was evidence that her taste in jewelry demanded something better. All I had was dime store junk. Then Chuck brought out a pair of undershorts which really caught her eye and the transaction was completed. The natives had some fancy canes to trade but would accept nothing less than a sheet or mattress cover, neither of which we had.

We visited another village where I picked up an ebony war club for a can of corned beef. I presented a can of salmon as a gift to the Chief. In his gratitude he presented me with a handmade fishing hook carved out of shell. The children were particularly taken with my hunting knife and I could have traded it for almost anything. When I took it out of the case, the sun struck the gleaming blade and the kids drew back with cries of amazement. At a third stop the children of the village gathered at the beach to meet us. As we came into the landing they broke into song. It was a catchy tune sung in the native language. We assumed it had primitive origins until we recognized it as their adaptation of "Wabash Cannon Ball." It was followed by joyful renditions of "You Are My Sunshine" and "God Bless America". I wondered if they had "God Save The Queen" in their repertoire for British visitors.

A few weeks later our ship was dispatched to the island of Malaita to visit an Australian coastwatcher. With Chief Sanders as coxwain, Chuck Bower and I went ashore, landing on a beautiful and isolated sandy beach. Once ashore we made our way through rows of towering palm trees to the top of a hill overlooking the harbor. Perched at the very top was a white bungalow with a wide cool veranda where we sat with the coastwatcher to conduct our business. By the time we got back to the ship native canoes were swarming all around us. Looking at the wizened old men who were paddling the canoes I wondered if any of them went back to the time, probably not that long ago, when white men were looked upon as tasty morsels for the stew pot.

After supper a small boat load of us visited a large native village on Auki Island near the entrance to the harbor. We were met by a bright native boy who undertook to be our guide. We had a good look inside the thatched huts and shook hands with the village chief. We watched a woman heating water by taking hot stones from a smouldering fire and dropping them into a pot of cold water. Throughout the tour we were followed by little naked children who kept asking "cigarette, Joe?". Everyone from babes in arms seemed to smoke. We persuaded the children to sing for us, so they sat down in a long row and sang to the accompaniment of a guitar. With natural and carefree gusto they sang haunting songs with unfamiliar harmonies and a strange syncopation. During one song a tiny boy who couldn't have been more than two began to dance. Soon he was joined by seven older boys who had the precision and rhythm of a chorus line. One of the older men told us that both the song and the dance told a story. To honor their guests they sang the Beer Barrel Polka and we all joined in.

By early 1944 the war in the Solomons had moved into a mopping up phase. Our assignments became more and more routine as we continued to ply from island to island, carrying supplies and occasionally troops. There were still Japanese strongholds on Bougainville, with Treasury Island off the Southern coast serving as a strategic supply and command center. We made frequent trips to Treasury and on one occasion I ran into Ray Shafer, Allegheny Class of '38 (destined to become Governor of Pennsylvania). Ray was the skipper of a PT boat based at Treasury. Ray invited me to come along on a torpedo run one night but I declined. I decided I was risking my neck enough without asking for more. Later in the war Ray's PT carried General Douglas MacArthur from Manila to a dramatic and symbolic landing on Corregidor when that island was finally liberated from Japanese occupation. Corregidor had been the site of a heroic stand by besieged American and Philippine troops in the spring of 1942.*

Ray Shafer was only one of many Allegheny and Meadville friends I ran across in the Solomons. Wally Hanson, an officer in Ray's PT

---

* *In the battle to recapture Corregidor, Lt. Shafer and Lt. Charles Adams risked their lives in the heroic rescue of twenty seven paratroopers who missed their targeted landing area. Author William Breuer documented their bravery in his book,* Devil Boats.

boat squadron, was an Allegheny Phi Delt, as were Larry Larson and Howard Beebe whom I saw occasionally. Chet Pardee, Lou Davies, and Chuck Cares were also from Allegheny. Lou was an officer on a fleet tanker, the U.S.S. Lackawana. I met both Lou and Chuck at the Iron Bottom Bay Club on Florida Island. Chuck was attached to the U.S.S. Alchiba, a cargo ship which after being attacked was saved from total destruction by a courageous crew.

An article "Through Hell To Glory" in Our Navy magazine described the adventure: "It was apparent that we could not beat out the flames and the Captain ordered the crew to abandon ship — except for those who volunteered to stick with him. Ensign Cares and his fighting second division kept unloading the bombs, working all through the night in spite of the smoke and the heat and the threat of impending death. By the next day they had emptied the hold that carried the bombs and eliminated the greatest danger of the whole ship blowing to bits." Chuck received a Presidential Unit Citation for his efforts. The ship was later salvaged and recommissioned as the U.S.S. Guadalcanal.

One day our ship was preparing to get underway from a mooring just off the coast of Guadalcanal. Just before we shoved off there was a message from the shore: "Pep would like to see Lt. Schultz." I rushed to get binoculars and there on the beach was Bruce ("Pepper") Martin, a high school and Allegheny friend from Meadville. He was waving his arms and hollering when finally some men on a raft picked him up and brought him out to the ship. We had about a two minute visit before we had to get underway but we talked fast and at least made a connection.

Another mini-reunion occurred when Bard Higgins arrived on the scene at a time when John McNair, Chuck Bower and I were all in the same port. Of twenty roommates who occupied the same large room at the Naval Midshipmen's school in Chicago, four of us became fast friends and continued to keep in touch. Chuck Bower, John McNair and I were ultimately assigned to APc Flotilla 5 while Bard had gone in another direction. We had not been together as a foursome since the time Bard's parents hosted a lavish evening for us at Earl Carroll's night club in Los Angeles. Bard was from Duluth, Minnesota and a graduate of Yale Law School. John was a University of Pittsburgh graduate from Pennsylvania.

With a few exceptions the crew of the "29" turned out to be just as capable as the the crew of the "37". There was Paul J. Conrad, Chief Boatswain Mate, a man in his late 20's, mature, respected, and a natural leader of men. Boggins, Storekeeper 1st Class, was a competent 30 year old Texan with prematurely grey hair who with Conrad was a steadying influence in maintaining harmony aboard the ship. There was a native American named White who had the most remarkable eyesight of anyone I have known. He was our best lookout and we depended on him when we were underway on the darkest nights. One of his favorite pastimes was spearing fish. He used to stand with the utmost patience until a fish came within range and with unfailing accuracy threw the spear to make the catch.

Just when we were beginning to get stir crazy we had a welcome respite from the routine of our assignments in the Solomons and the oppressive heat. We received orders to proceed to Noumea, New Caledonia for dry docking and maintenance. It was April of 1944 just one year after I had first visited Noumea on the APc-37. On the second visit Noumea took on the aura of a vacation resort. Compared to the Solomons it was heaven. Cool breezes and low humidity allowed us to sleep comfortably for the first time in months. Our chronic heat rashes disappeared. Everywhere there were vestiges of civilization which we had missed in the Solomons. Not only were there men and children, but women in large numbers, including Navy nurses, WACs and Red Cross workers. There was an abundance of fresh foods which we enjoyed only on occasion in the Solomons. There was big name entertainment. We enjoyed concerts by Eddie Peabody, the world's foremost banjo player, and John Carter, a tenor of the Metropolitan Opera. We returned to our base in the Russell Islands with a sturdy new washing machine, a new typewriter, a better radio and a hull cleansed of its barnacles.

During our stay in Noumea we learned that Chuck Bower was scheduled to return to the States and I was to take his place as Commanding Officer. We made the transition after we returned to the Russells. Floyd Eckert was promoted to Executive Officer and Jim Brown, an Ensign from suburban Philadelphia, arrived from the States to take over as Third Officer. Jim was 23 years old, married, and a graduate of Temple University. The most notable change in moving up to captain was in my quarters. I had a stateroom adjacent to the pilot house, all to myself. No longer did I have to share a

Crew of the APc-29. Back row left to right: Officers Floyd Eckert, Jim Schultz, and Jim Brown with Chief Boatswain's Mate Conrad and other crew members.

Black Gang (engineering crew) of the APc-29

cramped cabin with Floyd. Coincident with the change of command was the assignment of a new cook, replacing Stokes. His name was Descaunets and his French origins were reflected in his culinary skills. Our cuisine improved immediately. We were not surprised to learn that Descaunets was formerly a caterer at the South Shore Country Club in Chicago. One of the officers said "Every meal he serves looks like it was going to a party."

By the time I took command we were making regularly scheduled runs to Treasury Island. We usually moved at night through tricky reef ridden passages. Navigation was not one of Floyd's long suits, so I was often up most of the night directing our course through the narrow channels with one eye on the radar and the other on the silhouettes of nearby islands. Cigarettes and black coffee kept me awake. A squadron of P-38 fighter planes was based on Treasury and I learned that Roy Klapper, husband of Diane Dean Klapper, a distant relative by marriage, was stationed there as a P-38 pilot. I got in touch with Roy, invited him over for dinner, and he made an immediate hit with the crew. There was something dashing about Roy that appealed to the romantic in all of us. As we approached Treasury he would fly out to meet us, dip his wings and zoom back to the base to be there when we arrived. As we got better acquainted he made a show of reckless bravado, diving on the ship and skimming across the bow so low that the more timid members of the crew flattened themselves on the deck. That made him even more popular. Each time he would come aboard for dinner and we could be assured that Descaunets would prepare a gourmet feast.

Not long after I became skipper of the "29" our routine was broken by another trip in support of coastwatching activities on the island of Malaita. Malaita was one of the largest islands in the Solomon chain. It had been largely bypassed in the fighting, but it held small pockets of Japanese and remained a strategic outpost for the observation and rescue mission activities of the coastwatchers. On our expedition an Army camera crew was put aboard the ship to make a documentary of the trip. A sister ship accompanied us. Together we carried a month's supplies for one of the coastwatchers, Captain John Svensen, and the loyal natives who assisted him.

We were met at the beach by Captain Svensen, a tough burly Australian. He guided the two APc skippers up a hill to his residence, a frame plantation house typical of the area. It was late morning when we arrived and we settled comfortably in wicker chairs on a large screened-in porch. His home was the nerve center for his coast watching operations. Before the conversation got very far he challenged us to a drinking bout. He wanted to see how U.S. Navy officers could handle the traditional drink of the Australian Navy, Nelson's Blood, which we soon learned was brandy with a beer chaser. We accepted the challenge but coasted while he drank himself into a mild stupor. We then sat down to a lunch of tough undercooked chicken served by two black women nude from the waist up with flat pendulous breasts dangling dangerously close to our plates. The camera crew was not invited to lunch but the trip to Malaita and the reception at the beach was recorded on film. After returning to the States I had a private viewing of the film in Hollywood at the former Hal Roach studios which had been taken over by the Army's Documentary Film Division.

Improvements in our living conditions continued as supply lines were shortened and the area became less hazardous. A radio network was established, dubbed appropriately "The Mosquito Network". We began to get more recent movies, and mail from home arrived with more regularity. One day a cry went up that there were two women going by in a motor boat. We grabbed binoculars for a closer look and decided they were entertainers from a U.S.O. troupe. There were still occasional air raid alerts but the few Japanese that penetrated the Solomons Islands air space were taken care of by Allied night fighters. I exercised my prerogative as Captain to install a non-regulation 50 calibre machine gun on the flying bridge. Our Gunner's Mate had spirited it away from a dump for crashed airplanes. I never got to use it for its intended purpose, anti-aircraft fire, but it was great fun for target practice.

In early August 1944 I received orders transferring me back to the States for refresher training at the Small Craft Training Center in Miami. A new officer came aboard as my replacement and I left the Russells for Guadalcanal to wait for passage on a troop ship. It was the first time in fifteen months that I had set foot on Guadalcanal and the changes were striking. The port of Lunga had become a military city. A network of hard surface crushed coral roads had replaced the crude dirt roads we saw when we first arrived in May 1943. Street signs had appeared and traffic jams were the norm. While I waited for a ship,

Bob Hope brought his touring group of entertainers to the island. Frances Langford was among the featured performers. I attended the show as one of many thousands of enthusiastic servicemen who crowded the outdoor theater. The applause was thunderous.

Fortunately a new acquaintance who was also awaiting transportation learned that an aircraft carrier was in port and leaving the next day for San Diego. He knew the ship's captain and persuaded him to let us go along as passengers. Because we took a long Southern route to avoid submarines the trip took several weeks, but it gave me a welcome rest from responsibilities of any kind. We sunbathed on the flight deck and napped in the afternoons. The ship had a good library and I had the time to read such tomes as "Anthony Adverse" and "The Brothers Karamazov".

One morning before dawn the ominous sound of "general quarters" rang through the ship and we immediately thought of Japanese submarines. I raced for the ladders that would take me several levels up to the flight deck, the passengers' assigned post in emergencies. In the scramble to reach the top someone kicked me in the forehead, inflicting my only wartime wound. Once we were assembled on the flight deck the Captain announced that it was only a drill. The ship's name was "Altamaha" which we were told was an Indian name for leaky canoe. It nevertheless delivered us to San Diego without incident.

The Home Front Experience

Landing in San Diego after eighteen months overseas was a downer. Call it culture shock, whatever, but as we walked the streets and toured the night clubs, it seemed as though there was too much "business as usual". We wondered if people knew or cared that there was a war going on. After a few days we had our answer. They did. Evidence was all around — ration stamps, food scarcities, restricted travel, U.S.O. Clubs, and constant reminders on the radio and cinema news reels. I was soon headed East for a twenty day leave on a train crowded with service personnel.

When the Erie Limited rolled into the Meadville railroad station there was a delegation to meet me. Not only my parents and sister, Laurana, but my future wife, Dorothy Koster. Dorothy was also in the Navy. She had left her job as a librarian at Hamilton College to join the WAVES in November 1943. After six weeks of basic training she went to a school at the Naval Air Station in Lakehurst, New Jersey to become a specialisit in weather observation and forecasting. Graduating as an aerogra-

Dorothy Koster poised for take-off to make weather observations. Note weather instruments mounted on the left wing.

pher she was then assigned to the Aerography Office at the Jacksonville, Florida Naval Air Base. There she sometimes donned a parachute, helmet and goggles to go aloft in an open cockpit plane to make weather observations. By the time she met me in Meadville she was working in a Navy communications unit in Washington, D.C. She had taken a weekend off to be on hand when I arrived back from the South Pacific. It was a wonderful surprise.

After the reunion with Dorothy and the family , I was on another train, this time to Miami. My orders read to report to the Small Craft Training Center for a retread program designed to equip me and others for assignments of greater responsibility. There was a B.O.Q. (Bachelor Officers' Quarters) at the Center, but as a two-striper I had the option of living off the base. I moved into an apartment in Miami Beach with Carl Noyes and Robin Williams, former APc officers I had known in the Solomons. It was a second floor apartment in a two story garden complex known as Picaddilly Manor. Navy officers occupied most of the apartments and their peccadillos prompted some of our friends to call it Passion Manor.

The idea that we lived in Passion Manor was reinforced by our voluptuous landlady, a much older woman then in her forties. We had no phone in the apartment, but she was generous enough to let us use her phone for both incoming and outgoing calls. One morning she hollered up the stairs to tell me that I had a phone call. When I entered her living room she was sitting casually in a chair, stark naked, reading a newspaper.

The advanced SCTC program which I attended was rigorous. There were classes every day from eight to five with study periods in the evening. The subjects were navigation, tactics, gunnery, damage control, communications and computerized controls. The rugged schedule interfered with my social life, but I managed to get to the beach on weekends and sample the Miami Beach night life which was at full flower during the war. As part of the damage control training we went aboard a broken down ship where actual battle conditions were simulated with surprising reality. In the course of one morning we were torpedoed, mined, bombed and strafed. Water poured through holes as more and more leaks developed. It was our job to repair the damage. At times it seemed hopeless as the compartments were flooded with water, but we managed to plug the leaks, wetter but wiser.

Another practical exercise was our introduction to C.I.C. (Combat Information Center), a computerized command center then being installed on the Navy's larger fighting ships. It was a fascinating new development but sufficiently complex that some of the officers held to the notion that C.I.C. stood for "Christ I'm Confused". A segment of our class boarded a destroyer escort for several days of cruising down the Florida coast to Key West and back. While closeted in a room full of high tech equipment we took turns programming torpedo attacks on a companion ship which accompanied us. We actually launched dummy torpedoes and I had the thrill of tracking my torpedo on radar as it hit the target.

With the start of "the season" in Miami Beach we lost our inexpensive digs to a renter from the North who was willing and able to pay seasonal rates. Forced to find a new home I paired up with Chuck Bower, my former colleague from the APc 29, who was completing his training at the S.C.T.C. We located comfortable rooms in a home owned by a fascinating woman, Lily Martin. Mrs. Martin was born of Scottish parents in South Africa and gained international recognition as a pioneer in the fledgling aviation industry. In 1913 she became the first woman pilot to fly over water. She and her husband, a noted airplane designer, were the first to fly an airplane into Alaska. Her husband later founded The Martin Company which became part of Martin Marietta. Mrs. Martin was a wonderful landlady who entertained us with tales of her exploits and pampered us with clean linens every day and snacks at bedtime. She even had a dinner party in our honor.

In late November I completed the training and spent five leisurely days at the posh Tatum Surf Club, waiting for word of my next assignment. The club was private but open to Navy officers. My only responsibility was a daily phone call to learn whether my orders had come through. A telephone on a palm tree next to the pool was a convenient place to make the daily call. My brief but glorious sojourn came to an end with orders transferring me to San Pedro, California. There I was to join a crew in training for assignment to the U.S.S. PC-804 which was under construction at the Commercial Iron Works in Portland, Oregon. I was slated to be Executive Officer on the ship and in that capacity was given immediate responsibility for the crew which was being assembled in San Pedro. My transit time was limited but I made a hurried trip to Meadville, stopping for a day in

```
                      U. S. NAVAL TRAINING CENTER        DEC 3 1944
                           MIAMI, FLORIDA
        NC130/P16-4/00(AS)


        FROM:              THE COMMANDING OFFICER.
        TO:                LIEUT. JAMES R. SCHULTZ, D-V(G),USNR,141976.  —
                           ENSIGN TERRY F. YARGER, JR., D-V(G),USNR,330895.
                           ENSIGN HAROLD P. BODENSTAB, E-V(S),USNR,340548.
                           ENSIGN ROBERT A. MACDOWELL, D-V(S),USNR,392631.

        SUBJECT:           CHANGE OF DUTY.

        REFERENCE:         (A) BUPERS DESPATCH ORDERS DATED 1 DEC. 1944.

             1.            REFERENCE (A) IS QUOTED HEREWITH FOR YOUR
        INFORMATION AND COMPLIANCE:

             "LT JAMES R SCHULTZ DVG 141976 ENSIGNS TERRY F YARGER
             JR DVG 330895 HAROLD P BODENSTAB EVS 340548 ROBERT A
             MACDOWELL DVS 392631 ALL USNR HEREBY DETACHED FROM TEMP-
             ORARY DUTY UNDER INSTRUCTION AT NAVTRACEN MIAMI FLO AND
             FROM SUCH OTHER DUTY AS MAY HAVE BEEN ASSIGNED PROCEED
             TO ROOSEVELT BASE TERMINAL ISLAND SAN PEDRO CALIF AND
             REPORT TO CO SMALL CRAFT TRAINING CENTERFOR TEMPORARY
             DUTY UNDER INSTRUCTION CONNECTION PC 804 X WHEN DIRECTED
             BY CO SCTC SAN PEDRO CALIF DETACHED FROM TEMPORARY DUTY
             UNDER INSTRUCTION PROCEED TO PORTLAND ORE AND REPORT TO
             SUPSHIP WILLIAMETTE IRON AND STEEL CORP FOR TEMPORARY
             DUTY CFO PC 804 AT COMMERCIAL IRON WORKS PORTLAND ORE
             AND DUTY ON BOARD WHEN COMMISSIONED REPORTING BY LTR
             COMTHIRTEEN AND COTCPAC SUBORCOMD SEATTLE WASHN X SEVEN
             DOLLARS PER DIEM ACCORDANCE ART 2501 4D NTI"

             2.            THIS IS CERTIFIED TO BE THE ORIGINAL DESPATCH
        ORDER.

             3.            DELIVERED AND DETACHED. PROCEED AND CARRY
        OUT BASIC ORDERS.

                                        B. R. HARRISON


                                        W. F. COLTON,
                                        BY DIRECTION.
```

*Orders assigning me and Ensigns Yarger, Bodenstab, and MacDowell
to the PC-804*

Washington to visit Dorothy. Then I boarded a train for Los Angeles
and on arrival plunged into a hectic round of activity.

Up at 6:00 A.M., calisthenics, a quick breakfast, round up the crew by
7:00 and off to classes and workshops which lasted all day. So went
the daily routine after I checked into the Small Craft Training Center
at Roosevelt Base on Terminal Island, San Pedro. In a round of intro-

ductions I got acquainted with the other four officers and 60 enlisted men who comprised the crew. In addition to the Captain, Alyn Jones, there were Ensigns Terry F.(Ted) Yarger, Jr., Harold P. Bodenstab, and Robert A. MacDowell.

A 23 year old from Minneapolis, Ted Yarger had left the University of North Carolina to enter the Navy's flight training program. When he failed to get his wings he attended Midshipmen's School and was commissioned a line officer. After a brief tour of duty in Panama he returned for further training at the Small Craft Training Center in Miami. He and his wife Marge were married in August 1944 but she remained in Miami when he headed west to join the crew of the 804.

Bob MacDowell, also married, had a background similar to Ted's. He had recently graduated from Midshipmen's School as a line officer followed by training at the S.C.T.C in Miami. Hal Bodenstab who was single was to be our Engineering Officer In a sense all of us were on probation until we proved that we could measure up to the requirements for PC duty. That gave us the opportunity to weed out some potential "bad apples", including a couple who persisted in going AWOL.

After a week of orientation I was dispatched to San Diego for two weeks of anti-submarine training at the West Coast Sound School. It involved the tracking of submarines with sonar equipment. Half the program was devoted to seagoing exercises which we approached as competitive games. It was one of the most enjoyable of my training experiences. Not so enjoyable but a critical part of the training was a one day session at Fire Fighting School. I was the only officer in a group of sailors attending the session so the tough Navy instructor, who was not an officer, took delight in posting me at the nozzle position of the hose. With a team of five enlisted men behind me and the instructor bringing up the rear I was pushed into a roaring inferno. Our laboratory was a large blockhouse with no windows, built to simulate the bowels of a ship. As we moved slowly into the building, flames were all around us. We no sooner extinguished flames in front of us than they sprang up in back of us. We were too busy to be terrified but that would have been an appropriate emotion had we thought about it. The instructor told us to "stay cool" which was hard to do when we were dripping with perspiration from the heat. The lesson learned was not to panic and it was a valuable one.

The training continued at an intensive pace. There were seagoing runs to learn ship handling and seamanship and, as the program ended I took a night train to San Francisco to attend a one week course in damage control. Training with the crew brought us together as a team and paid big dividends later on. As the PC-804 neared completion at the Commercial Iron Works shipyard the officers were needed to oversee the outfitting of the ship. Four of us were dispatched to Portland while the fifth officer, Ensign Bob MacDowell, stayed in San Pedro with the crew. They were scheduled to join us when the ship was commissioned.

When I arrived to check in at the venerable Benson Hotel in downtown Portland, the desk clerk handed me a note to call Alyn Jones immediately. Alyn was scheduled to be Captain of the 804. When I reached Alyn he told me not to check in but instead to get a taxi and come to the Waverly Country Club, one of Portland's finest. He had made a deal for the four of us to stay at the club until our ship was commissioned. It was an ideal set-up. The Waverly had a few spacious bedrooms on its second floor and gave us membership privileges while we were there. The only other resident guests were several Wave officers and we had no objection to their presence. We were pampered by the members who invited us to their parties and made us feel at home in the community. Portland rolled out the red carpet for the Navy during World War II and we were given ample opportunity to sample its hospitality. Alyn Jones said that he felt like a debutante. We had many more invitations than we could accept so it was probably a good thing when the pressures of work began to interfere with the social schedule. It was tough duty!

The U.S.S. PC-804 was commissioned on February 6, 1945 with all the pomp and ceremony accorded a battleship. It was a big event in Portland with a record attendance, including families of some of the crew. A preacher from Pendleton, Oregon, father of our Yeoman 1st Class, gave the invocation. After the ceremony we held open house and guests toured the ship. The 70 year old mother of our Chief Machinist's Mate was among them. In a letter I wrote that "in spite of her age she insisted on climbing down the steep ladder into the engine room to see where her son worked". With the perspective of a senior citizen I would modify that statement today.

*U.S.S. PC-804 commissioning ceremony at Commercial Iron Works, Portland.
I am standing stiffly at attention, second from the right.*

U.S.S. PC-804, launched and ready for sea

The PC-804 wasn't a battleship or a cruiser or even a destroyer but it was sleek and fast with the silhouette of a fighting ship. It was a far cry from the big wooden APc tub for which I developed such affection during my previous tour of duty. The 804 was a 173 foot submarine chaser, 280 tons, with a complement of 65 men, including 5 officers. It carried a 3" gun on the bow, 1 forty millimeter and 4 twenty millimeter anti-aircraft guns, and depth charge launching racks on both the stern and the bow. Although we had the option of living ashore I moved aboard ship on the day of the commissioning. I liked the idea of a short commute — from my bunk to the desk in my stateroom. At the outset each day was a blur of organizing activity from early morning until after midnight. Starting with the assignment of bunks and lockers to publishing the daily routine, preparing the weekly schedule, revising the battle bill, putting the finishing touches on the ship's organization book, ordering additional supplies and educational materials, it was a round of routine and often bureaucratic activity. The fun began later when, with the organization in place and systems established, we left port and headed into the Pacific.

With the ship fully provisioned, the equipment installed and tested, the crew assembled and functioning, we sailed down the Columbia River in late February 1945. Our destination was San Pedro where we were to undergo seagoing trials. After a peaceful ride on the river it was a jolt to come to the Columbia River bar, one of the most turbulent patches of coastal water in the world. Here is my account of riding through those waters:

> "I found the salt air and the rolling waves refreshing after my tour of duty ashore. After the many months spent aboard my last ship, I thought I had become accustomed to riding a cork in rough seas, but the first few hours away from land proved that I had lost my sea legs. The junior officers and many of the crew were over the rail for several days, and even I, the old salt, must admit that I lost a portion of the first day's breakfast. We sailed through a minor storm and I discovered that a PC is eligible to compete anytime with an APc for an oceanic rough riding cup. Willliams, one of our quartermasters and an APc graduate, agrees with me; he is still green from

the experience. Physically it had little effect on me and I was one of the few who slept like a log despite the tossing of the ship. While standing watches on the flying bridge I was often astonished to find myself face to face with the water even though my two feet were planted firmly on the deck."

When we arrived in San Pedro we were greeted with startling news. The PC-804 was to be converted into a Communications Control Ship. We were diverted to a construction yard where workmen ripped out bulkheads to make room for a sophisticated communications system and quarters for a team of seven communications experts. In the process we lost much of the space devoted to amenities which would have made life at sea more comfortable. The role of the Communications Control Ship was to participate in large scale amphibious operations as the communications focal point for the landing and deployment of assault troops.

The ship's conversion extended our stateside duty and gave me the opportunity to enjoy recreational opportunities and visit friends throughout the Los Angeles basin. We rode the big red interurban streetcars to Hollywood where we listened to some of America's greatest jazz musicians — Coleman Hawkins, Nat King Cole, Barney Bigard and others. One evening Katherine Wilson, a former Allegheny student, and I joined Bob MacDowell and his wife Helen to listen and dance to the big band music of Harry James in Long Beach.

I met the well known jazz musician, Ray Linn, on several occasions and had dinner with his mother, Mary, at their home in Beverly Hills. Mary was a childhood friend of my mother from Canton, Missouri. I had fished for catfish in the Mississippi with her son Ray when we were both kids visiting our respective grandparents. Ray became one of the foremost trumpeters of his day as a featured soloist with Tommy Dorsey and later the Jimmy Dorsey orchestra. After dinner with him one evening I escorted his girl friend to hear him play with Benny Goodman's orchestra at the Palladium in Hollywood.

Through a Meadville contact I was able to get tickets to some of the major radio shows emanating from Hollywood. One of them was the Edgar Bergen / Charlie McCarthy show. I talked with Mr. Bergen after the show and he reminisced about his days on the travelling Chautauqua circuit when my father as a Chautauqua superintendent used to introduce his ventriloquist act. We also visited the famous Trocadero night club where we saw Frank Sinatra, Zsa Zsa Gabor, Ava Gardner and other Hollywood luminaries.

One of the construction workmen stood out among the others as a gregarious and articulate exception to the hard hat stereotype. He made a point of getting acquainted with the officers and one day invited our captain, Alyn Jones, to his home in Santa Monica for dinner. Alyn declined but, without asking us, volunteered that Ted Yarger, our third officer in seniority, and I would be happy to come. Taking that as an order, Ted and I reluctantly agreed to go. At the end of a shift we climbed into the workman's sporty car and headed for his home. When we got there we found an extended family of Italianos and a table groaning with tempting pasta dishes. Abruptly at the end of the meal we were ushered by our workman friend and three of his burly male relatives into a late model Cadillac. We drove aimlessly through the streets of Sant Monica and vicinity for almost an hour, ending up at the palatial home of one of our escorts in Beverly Hills. With a minimum of conversation the four men settled down to a serious poker game while Ted and I watched. The bizarre sequence of events made us nervous, so we made excuses and started to leave. They countered by offering to drive us back to the ship, a distance of forty miles. Ted and I had no idea how we would get back on our own, but we were willing to try. We said "no thank you". They insisted and insisted and finally prevailed. All six of us got back into the Cadillac and started for San Pedro. It was a long ride. All I could think of were the movies I had seen where the "good guy" was "taken for a ride" and disappeared forever.

The game they were playing became apparent as we drove along. These guys, without a doubt members of the Mafia, were in the black market, a lucrative business in an era of wartime shortages. In ever so subtle ways they made it clear to us that it would be worth our while to funnel cigarettes, candy, and sundries from our ship's store into their distribution system. Unless we had had a tape recorder there was no way to prove their intentions and even then the language they used was so obscure that it may not have served as valid evidence. It was a relief when we finally arrived at the shipyard. They wanted to come aboard but this time we had the upper hand and said a polite but emphatic "no". Our friend the workman made another not so subtle approach to us the next morning but our reply scared him off. We reported the incident and a few days later he was not among the work crew.

During construction the ship's routine continued. The new equipment, extra crew members and rearrangement of quarters kept us so busy that Alyn and I often found ourselves burning the midnight oil. Alyn was a spit and polish officer who reveled in the pomp and ceremony of the Navy. Our ship was scarcely big enough to warrant such formalities, but Alyn did what he could to emulate battleship protocol. Wearing white gloves he held periodic Captain's inspections. He led the inspecting party. I followed one pace behind him and a half a pace to the left. The yeoman followed a half a pace to the right taking down notes. The officers in charge of departments followed behind me while we passed through their departments. For Alyn it was serious business. Fortunately I managed to keep a straight face.

Alyn and I got along well even though or perhaps because we operated with different styles. He was a Southerner from Georgia and an economics graduate of Georgia Tech. Socially he was a loner and difficult to approach. He kept to himself except when he was playing the role of Captain which he loved. By mid April the conversion was complete and we prepared for departure as a fully operational warship. At that point Alyn announced that he would not be going with us. Except for a rash on his hand he seemed to be in good health but he left the ship under orders for emergency hospitalization. His sudden departure led to much speculation. When we learned that he would not be returning there were cheers from the crew. His replacement, Lt. Victor A. Hampshire, an experienced officer with a warm outgoing personality, received an enthusiastic welcome.

A Stone's Throw From Tokyo

With conversion completed the U.S.S. PC-804 took on a new personality. It also received a new designation — the U.S.S. PC(C)-804. With state-of-the art communications equipment, the new communications team, and a crew that was happy to leave the shipyard we headed for Pearl Harbor. The trip was a far cry from my first crossing on the APc-37. The PC was sleek and cruised at almost twice the speed of the APc. The quarters were more crowded but there was more deck space and we had more conveniences. Instead of riding the waves we cut through the waves, giving us a smoother ride. Psychologically I was better prepared for the cruise than I had been when I left for the first time on the APc. My thoughts at the time were expressed in a letter : "I expect it is confidence combined with more knowledge of the places or type of places I will be seeing. The last time it was like sailing out into the vast unknown and it gave me an insecure feeling. Now I know more of what to expect and I don't feel any anxiety."

We no sooner arrived in Pearl Harbor than we were dispatched to Maui to participate in amphibious landing maneuvers. In two weeks of simulated landings we learned the destiny of the 804 in its new role as a communications control ship. The maneuvers were impressive. From well off shore battleships bombarded the beach to neutralize enemy positions. Their efforts were supported by waves of dive bombers. Next came the troop ships which lowered boats to carry army personnel ashore. The troop ship landing operations were directed by communications control ships such as ours. There was one communications ship for each beachhead. In practice all went well, but we speculated on the prospects of success in actual combat with the Japanese.

In the spring of 1945 Maui was a quiet unspoiled tropical paradise with a few small villages connected by narrow winding roads. Tourist development on Maui was a post World War II phenomenon. In a rare respite from our maneuvers we took the crew ashore for a picnic in a public park that stretched along a pristine beach. In the distance we could see snow capped mountains on the island of Hawaii. Through the influence of Commander Hunter who was aboard for the maneuvers we were able to tour the island in a

Plymouth sedan, stopping for an al fresco supper at a Navy beach club. There and elsewhere I continued to cross paths with many of my former shipmates and friends from home, including Paul Green and Art Nichols whom I had known in my high school days.

Vic Hampshire had quickly gained the respect and affection of the crew with his knowledge of seamanship and a happy-go-lucky personality. In contrast to my former skipper, Art Bergstrom, Vic was a laid back extrovert with a great sense of humor. He conducted a "Happy Hour" broadcast over the ship's P.A. system with a clever line of chatter while he introduced records and up-to-date news items from the ship's radio. Vic was a graduate of Westminster Junior College in Salt Lake City. As a full Lieutenant he outranked me even though he was slightly younger.

The sky fell in for Bob MacDowell during our Maui maneuvers. His wife, Helen, was a young war widow when Mac first met her in Miami. Her first husband had been a B-24 pilot and was listed as missing after his bomber was shot down over Burma. Helen traveled across the country talking to anyone who might know whether he had survived. Members of his squadron who saw his plane go down told her there was no chance he could have escaped alive. Finally the War Department pronounced him dead. Two months later Helen and Mac were married. The wedding took place in Long Beach just as Mac was assigned to the PC-804. As newlyweds they were a delight. Obviously head over heels in love, they radiated affection and charm. Helen adopted all of us as part of her extended family and we welcomed her as an ex-officio member of the officer complement. On one occasion Helen and Mac joined Ted Yarger and me for an evening at the Trocadero in Hollywood. That night Helen taught me how to do the Samba. Frances Langford was doing the same dance nearby and we decided we did equally well.

The news came in a letter from Helen to Mac. When Rangoon was liberated by the Allies, her first husband was found alive and well in a Rangoon hospital. She cabled him immediately: "Darling, I am so glad you are alive; will see you soon. I love you with all my heart." Then began an agonizing few days while she sorted out her feelings. She loved her second husband too, but finally she decided. "My marriage to Mac was wonderful", she said in an interview with Time Magazine. "Perhaps in some ways Mac was closer to me, but I know

International, Associated Press

HUSBANDS & WIFE
"Mac was wonderful . . . but Harold is the one I love."

Six months after Bob MacDowell's marriage dissolved, Mac and I are pictured riding in a pedicab in Shanghai, China.

now that Harold is the one I love." That was the essence of the message Mac received in his letter from Helen. Mac was devastated. With Vic Hampshire's support, working through the chain of command, he appealed unsuccessfully for a leave to visit Helen and plead his case. Meanwhile she went home to Portsmouth, Ohio to wait for Harold's return. The second marriage was annulled and Mac went back to work. It was a blow to all of us. A poignant note was added when Helen addressed a letter to Vic and to me. She poured out her heart, told of her initial indecision, the difficulty of making a decision, and asked that we take good care of Mac. The newspapers called it the modern Enoch Arden story, drawing on the parallel from Alfred Lord Tennyson's famous poem.

We left Pearl Harbor in mid-May and took a route much farther to the North than we had taken two years before on the APc. Hostilities had shifted to areas closer to Japan as the Allies relentlessly recaptured islands occupied by the Japanese. With a brief stop at Wake Island we proceeded to Guam where we were awed by the devastation we saw in what was left of Agana, the capital city. At that time there had been little time to rebuild but a brand new Coca Cola plant was in operation. The Armed Forces had their priorities.

Our next stop was Saipan to pick up and install some specialized equipment, including smoke screen generators. Saipan was scarred with evidence of the heavy fighting which took place on that heavily fortified island. When the Japanese were finally defeated many took to the hills and continued to harass Allied troops with guerilla tactics. We were impressed with the waves of B-29 bombers which took off from Saipan on their way to bomb Japanese cities. It gave us a feeling of confidence that the war in the Pacific could soon come to an end.

We spent two weeks on Saipan. Willard Price in his book "Japan's Islands of Mystery" described his first impression of the island: "The green island rose from the shore in gentle slopes and terraces. ...Saipan is a lovely isle of billowing cane fields edged with coconut palms, breadfruit and bananas, flame trees and tree ferns." We found it to be green and extensively cultivated but much of its original beauty had been marred by the ravages of war. Fortunately the flame trees remained in all their resplendent glory. They could be seen from some distance at sea, brilliant splashes of orange against the green landscape.

Leaving Saipan, my thoughts as we continued to sail through Northern Pacific waters were revealed in a letter to my parents:

> "Looking at the map of the Pacific, I am somewhat astonished to think that I have wandered so far from

familiar haunts into regions I scarcely knew existed
a year or two ago. The monotony which character-
izes life at sea has prevailed for many of the crew,
but some inner curiosity has kept me from the indif-
ference I see in others. Each sunset and each new
island are exciting. I try to gain a full appreciation
of the moment, just as I used to thrill at the skyscrapers in New York or a cool summer day at the
Bousson farm. There seems to be no reason why I
shouldn't be a tourist as well as a sailor."

There is no better place to view a sunset than from the deck of a ship.
The sky was often a splash of color in all directions as it faded from
a blazing orange to patterns of pale pink. With the ship gliding
through the water, gently rolling from side to side, it was a poetic
sight to watch the sun sinking beyond the horizon. One evening I
climbed up to the crow's nest to get a better view.

Cruising on the PC had advantages over the APc. The officers' quarters were cramped and stuffy, but we had more room to stretch our
legs on the open decks. Many nights I escaped from the stifling heat
of the cabin to the signal bridge where I could watch the stars and
feel the breeze as I drifted to sleep. Unlike the APc, the PC had
movies on board. Enroute to Guam we saw Betty Grable in "Coney
Island" and Gene Tierney in "Laura". I delved into literature again
after a year in which I had been too busy to open a book. I finished
"The Razor's Edge" by Somerset Maugham, "Strange Fruit" by
Lillian Smith, "The Bridge of San Luis Rey" by Thornton Wilder and
"Children of Abraham, a collection of short stories by Sholem Asch.
After reading "Strange Fruit" which painted a sordid but realistic
picture of negro conditions in the South I had a lively discussion
with John Bohannon who also read the book. John was from
Ashville, North Carolina. With his Southern drawl he commented
that "only a Damned Yankee" could have written it.

As the chief navigator for the ship I got up an hour before sunrise
every day to shoot the morning stars and plot our position on the
navigation chart. In the middle of the morning and again at noon I
took shots of the sun. At sunset I took star sights and by the time I
worked them out it was almost time for bed. When the sky was over-
cast we were forced to go by dead reckoning. In between naviga-

tional chores I ironed out personnel problems, ran emergency drills, conducted training exercises, read books and occasionally sunbathed. At 2000 (8:00 P.M.) word was passed over the P.A. system: "Now hear this, now hear this. All department heads lay your eight o'clock reports before the executive officer." These were routine reports on the condition of the ship which I consolidated into a report to the Commanding Officer. All of the formality, salutes, and "sirs" involved seemed a little absurd for such a small ship, but Vic Hampshire had been in the States long enough to become entangled in the maze of Navy regulations.

Ship's Cook First Class "Johnny" Ross was a former cook from the west coast fishing fleet. Tough and good natured he turned out good hearty food with no frills. Our meals were served in the wardroom by Wade, Officers' Cook First Class and Ruffin, Steward's Mate First Class. The two were a contrast in personalities. Ruffin was withdrawn and stoic. Wade was an extrovert with a good sense of humor. What we lacked was the tender loving care of their APc counterparts, but we were well nourished with no grounds for complaints.

One of the crew came down with the mumps while we were underway. With no logical way to isolate him, we set up an improvised bed in a life boat, shaded the boat with an awning and there he rested in state. Those in the crew who hadn't had mumps made a careful detour around the boat until he recovered. It was June and the weather was hot. We cooled the decks with water so that we could walk on them. One day we smelled burning rubber and discovered it was coming from one of the men's shoes. He had been sitting too long with his feet on the deck.

Shipboard humor often took the form of practical jokes. Early one morning Harris, our competent Yeoman First Class, made a request over the P.A. system: "Will the person who put the flying fish in my desk drawer please remove same immediately?" Our quartermaster, William C. Gosbee, was a tall gangly New England gothic who appears to the right of the ship's stack in the commissioning picture. He had enormous feet and was the subject of much hilarity among the crew. They accredited him with the huge footprints advertising the March of Dimes on Portland sidewalks. There was also talk of using his size 14 shoes as auxiliary lifeboats.

Calixto Florendo, our Filipino signalman, kept us amused with his good nature and razor sharp wit. When he spotted one of my former APc vessels, he shouted: "That's the ship I should be on. It's more my size." He was an expert signalman and went about his work with ferocious intensity. Because of his size he couldn't reach the signal light by standing on the deck, so he climbed up the light standard and wrapped himself around it monkey fashion. He sent blinker signals like streaks of lightning and when he received signals from another ship he had to peer around or underneath the light to see. Meanwhile he carried on a one way conversation with the signalman on the other ship. If the other fellow was not on the ball, he gave him hell. He was eager to get a crack at the Japanese and was probably the only member of the crew who looked forward to seeing Japanese planes. He wanted to be the first to get a shot at them. His home was on Luzon in the Philippines. He had had no word from his parents from the time of the Japanese invasion and was anxious to return. We were hoping to get him shore duty there.

Letters from home were eagerly anticipated, but they didn't always carry good news. There was an occasional 'Dear John' letter, but some were the grim and tragic reminders of the war we were fighting. One of our radiomen named Parkington opened a letter to learn that his younger brother, an Ensign pilot in the Navy, had been killed in the crash of his airplane. The message was cryptic with few details. Parkington had the fortitude to carry on, but he still cried a good part of the afternoon.

Other letters reflected the tribulations of life on the civilian front. My father, John Richie Schultz, wrote of his difficulties in trying to get from here to there on public transportation. As President of Allegheny College, he had been invited to officiate at the christening of the S.S. Allegheny Victory, a liberty ship named for the college which was scheduled to be launched in June 1945 at the Kaiser shipyards in Richmond, California. He flew from Pittsburgh to St. Louis and that is where the trouble began. He described the experience:

> "When we landed in St. Louis, the announcement was made to the passengers that the flight had been cancelled because of weather conditions in Kansas City. All planes from the East were being stopped at St. Louis, and they thought nothing would go out

before that afternoon. Priority passengers had piled up so that they were quite sure that no one without a priority would be able to go on for two or three days. They advised me to go by train to Kansas City in the hope that something would get up through the ceiling from there or that new flights would start. This hardly seemed likely to me, but I did not want to give up.

So I went to Kansas City. The trains are crowded to capacity, and I would have been unable to get across Missouri if I had not been able to bribe the porter on the chair car to let me sit in the observation end. At Kansas City there was neither plane nor train reservation available. I think they did what they could, but that was absolutely nothing. I was determined to find some way to make it. I went out to Union Station and stayed until the last train left that would get me in on Saturday. I got the passenger agent of the Union Pacific interested in my project and he personally checked every Pullman car to see if there was any loophole. We gave up on that at 9:15. Then he undertook to check every other train until 10:15. There was nothing available.

I thought I might get on the day coach and see if something would turn up, but he was sure that everything was tight as far as Denver, where we would not have been due until three o'clock the next afternoon. I had not been to bed the night before and had no sleep at all, and I was afraid to under take such a strenuous trip. The coaches were packed and jammed, with people standing in the aisles and vestibules, as tight as they can be packed in. I certainly hated to give up, but it seemed the only thing to do."

From Saipan we set a course straight for the island of Okinawa which the Allies had recently occupied with heavy resistance from the Japanese. As we neared the island we tuned into the armed forces radio station on Okinawa. It aired an entertaining mix of news and music, but the station identification, given each hour on the hour, carried an ominous reminder of our proximity to Japan: "This is WXLE, Okinawa, a stone's throw from Tokyo." Only a short distance from Japanese airfields to the north, Allied ships and military installations on Okinawa were vulnerable to nightly bombing attacks by kamikaze pilots. Desperate to stem the tide of advancing Allied forces, the Japanese had trained young pilots to undertake suicide missions against military targets. To the Japanese, kamikaze means "divine wind", but there was nothing divine in the mayhem they caused. With deadly accuracy the "kamikazes" flew their planes directly into Allied ships approaching or anchored in Okinawa bays. To counter the kamikaze strategy the Allies developed a chain of ships to patrol the Okinawa coast. Each ship had a segment of the coast to patrol. When a red alert signaled that Japanese planes were approaching, each ship fired up its smoke cannisters, creating clouds of smoke to obscure the ships and confuse the incoming pilots.

It was a bright sunny day and the water was dead calm when we rounded the southern tip of Okinawa and passed from the Philippine Sea into the East China Sea. If it had not been for gunfire on the island's rocky cliffs, the entire scene would have been one of peace and quiet. As it was, we were on the alert constantly, expecting each plane that appeared to be Japanese on a suicide mission. If we had been looking for action, which we weren't, we would have been disappointed. By the time we arrived in Okinawa, the only Japanese air attacks were launched under the cover of darkness. Each night only a few Nipponese planes were able to penetrate the heavy shield of shore based anti-aircraft fire and Allied air force night fighters. A muffled explosion and distant glow through the smoke screen was a signal that a kamikazi pilot had hit his mark.

When the PC(C) 804 arrived at Okinawa, it was immediately assigned to picket duty. We took our position along the northwest coast, cruising back and forth along a designated route. Night came and we tuned in to the battle frequency that kept us in touch with defense operations. Soon there was a radio report that Japanese planes were on the way. We listened and could hear the faint drone of aircraft engines in the distance. Then we heard the order: "All ships make smoke". We were prepared. We had picked up a supply of smoke cannisters in Saipan. Crewmen activated our cannisters but instead of smoke there were bright flames, illuminating our ship and the surrounding area. The next thing we heard was a gruff voice on the radio, "Who the hell is lighting up the place?" Keenly aware that we had become an inviting target, we managed to deep six the cannisters before the Japanese were overhead. From that night on we made sure that our cannisters made only smoke as they were supposed to do.

At times we were relieved from picket duty to refuel, pick up supplies and undertake special patrol or escort assignments. On one occasion we were dispatched to rendevous with another ship near Iheya Retto just north of Okinawa. As we approached the ship, it hoisted an unfamiliar flag signal. We opened the code book, located the signal and were startled to read: "Submerge three feet." Our reply isn't recorded, but the blooper lives on as a testimony to careless communications. The waters of Iheya were so clear and inviting that we went for a swim while we were in the area. All guns were manned on such occasions, just in case.

One day we skirted the southern tip of Okinawa on our way to Nakagasuku Wan which the Allies had renamed Buckner Bay. It was a major supply and command center for Allied operations, not far from Naha, the capital of Okinawa, a city of 60,000 which had been leveled by Allied bombing. On our way we passed close enough to shore to see our troops using tanks and flame throwers trying to rout the Japanese from the caves and rocky recesses which characterize the terrain of that area. Other expeditions took us to Ie Shima, Kerama Retto, Tori Shima, and Aguni Shima. Most of the islands were well populated with small villages and numerous well-cultivated farms. The villages were neat with attractive homes, all with thatched roofs. They were located for the most part in groves of shade trees. An occasional pagoda could be seen rising above the trees and against the neighboring hills were numerous tombs dotting the landscape. The countryside was a vibrant green and the slopes were terraced for irrigation purposes.

In mid-July there were reports of a typhoon headed for Okinawa. We tracked the storm as it approached and finally received orders to head for the open sea. We were the smallest of the Navy ships in the area expected to ride out the storm. Ships smaller than ours were directed to find shelter in protected coves and rivers. Following orders we headed in an easterly direction as fast as we could, but we couldn't outrun the storm. It began to descend with frightening fury.

The sky turned a dull dark yellow grey and winds screamed past the ship. The waves rose higher and higher until they were mountainous. As the storm grew in intensity the ship seemed to grow smaller. We were pitched and tossed around like an insignificant piece of driftwood.

When the full force of the storm hit us, torrential rains reduced visibility to near zero. The ship rode up on the crest of an enormous wave and plunged almost vertically down the other side, so steep a plunge that the twin screws were out of the water, lending an eerie noise to the cacophony of sounds that enveloped us. Reaching the bottom of one wave we looked up to see another arching over the bow. As it slammed down, the ship seemed to be momentarily submerged, surfacing to take yet another blow. With each wave the hull was pounded and the bulkheads groaned. One by one the food and ammunition lockers we had so carefully lashed to the decks were washed overboard. All of the life rafts were swept away. It was a rough ride, difficult to stand upright, and much too dangerous for anyone to go out on deck. With luck and the skill of our helmsman who kept us heading into the sea, we didn't capsize. It was twenty four hours of hell, but we made it through and blessed the Commercial Iron Works for making such a seaworthy ship.

When we returned to Okinawa we saw many of the smaller ships scattered high and dry along the beach. Okinawa had taken the full brunt of the typhoon and the damage was extensive. At least it gave us a respite from Japanese air attacks. They resumed as soon as the weather calmed, but not with the same frequency. The massive B-29 bombing attacks on Japanese airfields were beginning to take effect. The priorities for the services of the PC(C)-804 were shifting and we soon received orders to head for the Philippines, a staging area for Allied forces preparing for an invasion of Japan. The cruise from Okinawa to the Philippines turned out to be one of the most memorable of my four years of service in the Navy.

Human Torpedoes

Fresh from picket duty off the shores of Okinawa, the U.S.S. PC(C) 804 weighed anchor and headed south. The crew looked forward to a change of scene. They were joining other patrol craft to escort a merchant ship and seven LST's to the Philippines. The prospect of what promised to be a routine assignment was a welcome relief from many tense days and nights of anti-submarine operations. Gliding along under southern skies there was nothing to suggest that the Japanese menace might interfere with a cruise which every hour was putting more distance between our ship and the enemy in Japan. Two days later it was a different story.

July 24, 1945 started as a routine day. The sea was calm, the weather warm and sunny, and spirits were high as the convoy cruised off Formosa (present day Taiwan). The U.S.S. Underhill, a destroyer escort, was the lead ship. The PC(C) 804 was positioned on the starboard side of the convoy. Early in the morning the Underhill signaled that they were making ice cream. "Come alongside this afternoon and we'll have some for you." That would be a rare treat for the 72 men aboard the "804". An ice cream freezer was a luxury we didn't have.

At 0900 the Underhill came on the air with a more serious message. They reported a Japanese reconnaisance plane in the area and

U.S.S. Underhill, victim of a manned torpedo.

ordered all escort vessels to take anti-aircraft stations. The plane followed at a safe distance and finally left. It was a disturbing incident but we weren't overly concerned. The smooth waters, the sunshine and the promise of ice cream later in the day made it difficult to believe that there could be trouble ahead. That afternoon we learned the significance of the reconnaisance plane seen earlier in the day.

At 1359 (1:59 P.M.) we received a message from the Underhill: "We have sound contact. We are investigating. This is not a drill. Do not acknowledge." Four minutes later the Underhill reported: "Contact definitely not sub. We have a horned type mine. We will probably try to sink by gunfire. Close in and cover my gap while I handle this mine." At 1420 (2:20 P.M.) there was another message. "We have that same suspicious contact. It bears 330 degrees 2300 yards. Can you turn around and take a look at it? I will help to coach you on." Fifteen minutes later the Underhill radioed: "You are over our last point of contact." Almost immediately we picked up the same contact at a range of 1200 yards. Before we had a chance to drop depth charges we lost contact and slowed engines until we could pick up the sound again.

The "804" was almost dead in the water when one of the crew shouted "periscope on the port quarter!". Sure enough, there it was, moving steadily in our direction. As it approached, the periscope retracted. We watched, fascinated. Soon we peered into the crystal clear water to see a large Japanese submarine glide slowly under our hull. It was a moment of incredulity. In a reflex action, a gun turret on the port side opened fire but to no avail. When we regained sonar contact. we revved up the engines and at the proper moment released a series of depth charges. We could hear and feel the underwater explosions but were never sure we inflicted damage. At least for a moment the sub was on the defensive. As the officer in charge of sonar operations I was trying to remember all the things I learned at sonar school in San Diego. It was suddenly clear that this was the real thing.

Within minutes we looked ahead to see a midget submarine heading straight for our bow. It was skimming through the water at a speed of fifteen knots, much faster than conventional submarines and too fast for depth charge calculation charts to be of value. Shaped like a torpedo it carried an explosive charge and was guided by a kamikaze. The "804" put on a burst of speed, made a quick turn and managed to avoid it. Almost immediately a report came from the fantail: "Midget sub fast approaching directly astern." As we altered course the second sub missed us by inches. We were in the middle of a wolf pack of manned torpedoes, launched by the large "mother" sub which had passed beneath our ship.

The Underhill was having similar problems. At one point it dropped depth charges and claimed a direct hit on one of the subs. At 1450 (2:50 P.M.) the Underhill sent a message: "We are going to ram." We watched as it pursued one of the wolf pack and reported back to the convoy. "He is chasing a one man sub going like hell." We were never sure whether the Underhill fully understood how deadly a quarry it was pursuing. A few minutes later the Underhill exploded in a towering cloud of smoke and debris. It had been hit from the side by another of the suicide subs at its most vulnerable point beneath the bridge and close to its ammunition supply.

When the smoke cleared there was an awesome silence except for screams coming from the oily black surface of the water. Only the stern of the Underhill and a small section of the bow remained intact. We were amazed to see so many survivors standing on what remained of the deck, but our attention was focused on those in the water. There were bodies and parts of bodies but some were alive. The reaction of our crew was heroic. We lowered boats in a rescue effort. Several men jumped into the water, secured by rescue lines to the ship. One of these swimmers, Domingo Adams, a Seaman First Class from Port Arthur, Texas, was responsible for saving the lives of seven men. We pulled a total of 17 men from the water. Then we concentrated on the remaining survivors huddled on the fantail of the Underhill. Our first attempt to go alongside was aborted when we spotted a periscope and had to take defensive action. It was one of several times when we were forced to deal with the continuing menace of the wolf pack. When we had a solid sound contact it was standard procedure to drop depth charges from the stern or launch small rockets from the "mouse traps" located on each side of our bow. These rockets entered the water in a fan shaped barrage designed to bracket the sub and inhibit its maneuvers. With the "mouse traps" we could react more quickly and improve the odds for a hit. There was evidence that we may have scored on one of the attacks.

```
                EXCERPT FROM RADIO LOG OF U.S.S. PC-804 -- JULY 24,1945*        59
     1442                                     BELIEVE WE SAW PERISCOPE ON  PORT QUAR
                                              TER WE ARE TURNING AROUND TO REGAIN
                                              CONTACT
                                              WE NOW HAVE CONTACT REQUEST PERMISSION
                                              TO ATTACK
                                              PERMISSION GRANTED

                                              R WE ARE COMING OVER
     1450      MM 18 V PROSPER 4              WE ARE COMING OVER TO HELP, OUT
               V MM 18                        OUR SOUND GEAR NOW BACK IN COMMISSION
               V MM 18                        WE ARE GOING TO RAM
               V PROSPER 4
                                              WE HAVE LOST SOUND CONTACT WE ARE MAKING
                                              CONTACT ON WAKES
               V PROSPER 4                    HAVE REGAINED CONTACT AM GOING IN FOR
                                              A RUN
               VIA TREPAN 2                   MM 18 IS GOING IN FOR ANOTHER RUN
                                              HE IS ON (QOTO) 3000
               VIA TREPAN 2                   THERE ARE TORPEDOES IN THE WATER KEEP
                                              A SHARP LOOKOUT
                                              HE IS CHASING A ONE MAN SUB GOING LIKE
                                              HELL
     1510                                     ONE MAN SUB GOING ABOUT 15 KNOTS
               SPANKER 46 V PROSPER 4         MM 18 BLEW UP WE ARE GONG ALONGSIDE TO
                                              HELP
               PROSPER 3 V PROSPER 4          PLEASE GIVE US AID IMMEDIATELY
               V PROSPER 3                    R OUT
               PROSPER 3 V PROSPER 4          PICK UP A DOCTOR FROM ONE OF THE GANG
     1515      XXXXXXX V PROSPER 3            R WAIT
               V COCRO 7                      WE HAVE A DOCTOR ABOARD COME ALONGSIDE
               V TREPAN 2                     241518/1 HAVE U REPORTED ACCIDENT IF NOT
               V PCE 872                      WE WILL MAKE REPORT ON RADIO
               V PROSPER 4                    U CAN REPORT THE ACCIDENT
     1520      V TREPAN 2                     R OUT
               PROSPER 3 V PROSPER 4          KEEP A SHARP LOOKOUT ON THE WAY BACK
                                              HERE FOR TORPEDOES IN WATER
     1525      V PROSPER 3                    R OUT
               V TREPAN 2                     GIVE US DETAILS ON ACCIDENT SO WE CAN
                                              MAKE REPORT
               V PROSPER 4                    R OUT
               SPANKER 46 V PROSPER 4         MM 18 CHASING ONE MAN SUB MADE SHARP
                                                 TURN TO RIGHT AND BLEW UP X (15081)
                                              BOW BLOWN OFF X BOW AND STERN STILL
                                              AFLOAT
               V TREPAN 2                     WHAT WAS CAUSE OF EXPLOSION
     1533      V PROSPER 4                    CAUSE BY RAMMING ONE MAN SUB-MARINE
               V TREPAN 2                     DO U THINK IT ADVISABLE TO ASK FOR
                                                 FURTHER AID X DO U FOR CONVOY X IS SO
                                              WE WILL ASK FOR IT WHEN SENDING OUT
                                              REPORT X DO U NEED ANY FURTHER AID FOR
                                              COCO COLA
     1535      V PROSPER 4                    R OUT
               V PROSPER 4                    AFFIRMATIVE X SEND PROSPER 3 AND ONE
                                              OTHER VESSEL
               V TREPAN 2                     DO U MEAN TO REQUEST AID FROM ANY
                                              SHORE STATION
               V PROSPER 4                    R WAID OUT
     1540      TREPAN 2 V PROSPER 4           WE ARE PICKING UP MEN NOW BELIEVE
                                              SUBS STILL IN AREA
                *
                MM 18 was the code name for U.S.S. Underhill
                Prosper 4 was the code name for U.S. PC-804
```

Excerpt from radio log of U.S.S. PC-804 — July 24, 1945.

When we returned from the first of these diversions we were able to transfer thirty of the most seriously wounded men from the stricken vessel. A 21 year old Pharmacist's Mate who survived the blast had set up a make-shift dressing station on the fantail of the Underhill. He and an assistant ministered to others whose injuries were not so serious or were too serious for them to be moved. Meanwhile two PC escorts from the convoy had been dispatched to assist us. One of them carried the doctor we had requested at the time of the explosion. They arrived on the scene shortly after 1700 (5:00 P.M.). Along the way they also had to deal with enemy sub contacts and reported that there were three subs still in the area. They removed the remaining members of the crew from the Underhill except for a skeleton force which hoped to salvage what was left of the ship.

There was feverish activity aboard the "804" as we continued to stay on the alert for more sub attacks. Meanwhile we converted the mess hall into a hospital ward and operating room. Responsibility for treatment of the casualities rested on the shoulders of a single enlisted man, Lesley E. Mann, Pharmacist's Mate First Class, from Glasgow, Montana. Many of the casualties were in critical condition from severe burns, concussions, fractures and hemorrhages. Mann administered medical aid to all of them and saved all but two of the most hopelessly injured. The doctor we requested stopped first to attend to some critically injured patients aboard the Underhill. When he finally arrived aboard the "804" it had been seven hours from the time of the explosion. His arrival was a welcome relief for Pharmacist's Mate Mann who had four patients needing amputation.

We tried to tow the after section of the Underhill but it became a futile effort as it settled more deeply into the water. Our next option was to sink what could become a serious navigational hazard. It wasn't easy. With our 3" gun we lobbed shell after shell into the stern. It wasn't until we moved in at close range that it finally sank. It was approaching midnight when we finally regrouped with the other escorts and set out at top speed for the Philippines. We had the doctor and 13 stretcher cases on board. When the final tally was taken there were 109 missing or dead and 126 survivors and wounded. Only four officers survived. The Captain and most of the senior officers had been on the bridge which suffered the direct impact of the kamikaze's hit.

Throughout the episode the crew of the "804 performed with remarkable composure and efficiency. There was no sign of panic and no outward manifestation of the fear they must have felt. We knew that at any minute we could meet the fate of the Underhill, but we were too busy to worry about it. We were running on adrenalin. I remember that I was tense and my mouth was very dry. None of us had had any food for hours, but we weren't hungry. There were no thoughts of the ice cream we never received from the Underhill. The reality of what we had been through didn't register until the next morning.

One of the survivors was 19 year old Larry D. Downs, Machinist Mate Third Class, from Pittsburgh, Pennsylvania. He had been aboard the Underhill from the time of its commissioning in November, 1943. On our way to the Philippines we had a chance to talk about the places we both knew so well in western Pennsylvania. On the chance that he would soon be returning to the States I wrote to my father suggesting that he contact Larry to get a first hand account of our experience. They exchanged letters in late September and a few weeks later both my mother and father had dinner with Larry in Pittsburgh. Downs had no addresses of those who were lost, but in a newspaper article he and his father, Lloyd Downs of the Pittsburgh police force, offered to help any parents in the area whose sons were among the missing.

Our destination was the island of Samar on the eastern side of Leyte Gulf in the Philippines. The Allies had established a major base around the shores of Leyte Gulf to be used as a staging area for a massive assault on Japan. There were also medical facilities to treat the wounded we had on board. When we arrived, Vic Hampshire, skipper of the "804", and I were whisked off to be debriefed by Naval Intelligence. An attack by kamikaze subs was a new and deadly development in the war at sea. Five days after the Underhill incident, the heavy cruiser, Indianapolis, was torpedoed and sank north of the Philippines with the loss of 884 lives. There was speculation that it too may have been the victim of manned torpedoes.

Because of censorship the story of the Underhill didn't hit the newspapers until the fall of 1945. By that time the PC(C)-804 was based in Shanghai and the war was over. The English language Shanghai Herald broke the story with a headline that read: "Heroic Men Of

Sub-Chaser in Port Saved 47 Survivors From Ship During Suicide Attack" An enterprising newsboy showed up at our ship with a stack of papers right off the press. He quickly sold out the entire lot for 50 cents apiece. Members of the crew were clamoring for more, so the boy returned with another stack, but this time the price was one dollar. He was a young and early practitioner of market economics. I often wondered how such a budding entrepreneur fared under the suppression and constraints of communism.

Japanese Surrender

After the scuffle with human torpedoes, it was a relief to be in the relative calm of Leyte Gulf. It offered a respite from the hazards of enemy confrontation, if only for a short time.

The arrival in Leyte Gulf turned into "old home week". There was such an assemblage of ships that the odds were in favor of bumping into a few friends but I wasn't prepared to see so many familiar faces. One of the first was Warren Winkler, from Meadville and Allegheny and a Phi Delt fraternity brother. As an officer on the Charles Carroll, an attack personnel carrier, Warren had seen duty in the European theater where his ship had participated in the landings on Normandy and Naval operations in the Mediterranean. Subsequently the Charles Carroll was reassigned to support operations in the Pacific. Warren's time in Leyte Gulf was limited but it gave us an opportunity for a brief visit. Shortly after he sailed I ran into Bob Thomas, a close friend who had grown up across the street from me in Meadville and also went to Allegheny where he joined the same fraternity. He was an officer on the Anne Arundel, a personnel carrier which like the Charles Carroll had served in the Normandy invasion and operations in southern France and Italy. The Ann Arundel anchored not far from the 804 for about a week. In that time Bob and I were able to visit back and forth a number of times, reminiscing and catching up on the latest news. One day Bob took a cruise aboard the 804 when we had to make a short trip across the harbor.

A number of former APc skippers were in the area and we got together for a nostalgic reunion. Art Bergstrom, newly assigned as the Executive Officer on a destroyer, was among them. We dined on each others ships and met occasionally at the Officers' Club where I continued to run into others I knew. Ed Fuld whom I had followed from the Solomons to the refresher school in Miami surfaced in Leyte Gulf as captain of a sea-going tug. He invited me to come over one evening to have dinner with Nathaniel Benchley, an officer from another PC whom I had met previously at the Officers' Club. "Nate" Benchley was a very funny guy who entertained us with jokes and witticisms which reflected his heritage as the son of the famous humorist, Robert Benchley. After the war "Nate" followed in his father's footsteps as an author and raconteur. His son Peter carried on the family tradition with a series of successful books, including "Jaws" which was a box office hit in the movie version.

When we arrived in the Philippines we entered into preparations for the landing on Japan and the first opportunity to function as a communications control ship. It was the role for which the 804 had been destined following its conversion in San Pedro. The work of the control ships had been described in a magazine article, "Traffic Cops of Invasion". It was an apt and descriptive title. With Leyte Gulf as a major staging area it was an exciting place to be.

The signals changed dramatically on August 6, ten days after we arrived from Okinawa. On that day a B-29 dropped an atomic bomb, the first ever used in warfare, on the port city of Hiroshima in southwestern Japan. The effect was devastating. Thousands were killed and injured. Industrial, commercial and port facilities were destroyed and sixty thousand homes were leveled. The Armed Forces Radio Station was full of the news all day, giving rise to rampant speculation and hope among the crew. Would there be more bombing? How long could the Japs hold out? How soon would we be going home? On August 9 the Allies dropped a second atomic bomb, this time on Nagasaki, leveling much of the city and harbor area. The next day Russia declared war on Japan in a thinly disguised effort to cash in on the spoils of war when it looked like a sure thing that the Allies would win. The news that night confirmed what we had been hoping. It was nine o'clock at night and we were sitting in the wardroom eating cantaloupe ala mode. The radio music was interrupted with a major news item: "The Japanese announced that they are willing to surrender."

Within seconds after the announcement everyone bounded up to the open decks, cheering wildly, jumping up and down, singing and hugging each other. The sky in all directions was ablaze with roving searchlight beams. Rockets and flares of every description and color were raining down on the harbor. Not to be outdone we expended our entire supply of colorful signal flares and star shells. There were over 2000 ships in Leyte Gulf that night and every one joined in the celebration. It was a glorious and emotional moment — one that we had all been waiting for. Our exhilaration was enhanced by what seemed to be an unlimited supply of booze. Where it came from I

With news of the Japanese surrender, this spectacular pyrotechnic display erupted from the 2000 ships assembled in Leyte Gulf on August 10, 1945.

really didn't want to know because Navy regulations prohibit liquor on commissioned vessels, except for medicinal purposes. Not only was the medicinal supply consumed that night but the spirits which came out of the woodwork as well. After the initial excitement I retreated to the bridge and stood there alone. Peace at last. It didn't seem possible.

Two days later we sailed north to the Naval Base at Subic Bay on the island of Luzon. It was a scenic trip through a narrow passage with hills and tropical vegetation so close on both sides that we could almost reach out and pick the coconuts. Quaint little native villages were situated on the water's edge and native canoes scooted back and forth across the channel. The natives were so curious and eager to be friendly that they came perilously close to the ship to smile and wave a greeting. The crew brought out the few chairs we had and sat back leisurely watching the scenery go by. Although it was interesting, it wasn't so restful for Vic and me. We were busy dodging reefs and tiny islands on into the night, but we enjoyed one of the most vividly colorful sunsets I have ever seen.

The euphoria of the Japanese peace overature lasted for several days. Then we began to wonder and worry. It had been four days from the time the Japanese expressed their willingness to surrender. Washington had made a counter-offer setting forth surrender terms, but there had been no further word. Finally President Truman announced that the terms were acceptable to both sides. The word reached us early in the morning of August 15 and unleashed a second celebration almost as spectacular as the first. It was not quite so boistrous but there was a steady din of noisy jubilance. Vic Hampshire, exercising his prerogative as Captain, stood in the pilot house blowing the siren and the whistle at the same time. He stayed there until Florendo came running in and asked if he please might blow them. All the ships in the harbor started shooting off fireworks and they were still going off well into the night. Streams of yellow, red, purple, green and blue smoke trailed across the sky from smoke flares. It was a beautiful sight.

I expressed my thoughts in a letter to my parents:

> "The war is over." "Those few words mean so much that it is taking a long time for them to sink in. Three and a half long years of hoping and wondering, of separation and worry, and of sorrow and death for some, are over. The separation will continue for a few months, I suppose, but with the fighting over the worry should be gone. The end has seemed so far away for so long that I have to pinch myself to realize that peace has come. I hope it will be a lasting peace as the diplomats say, but I wonder. I feel much more than I am able to express."

Within days Admiral Nimitz announced a point system to determine eligibility for discharge. Points were given for months of Navy service, age and dependents. When I added up my score at age 25 with no family, the magic date was 1948. We didn't even have a slogan for that year. The slogan we were counting on was "Home Alive In '45". If not, it was "Back To The Sticks In "46". Fortunately the system was later revised to include time overseas. With my 22 months of South Pacific duty, that moved me up on the list. As soon as the point system was activated we shipped off three of our crew who were qualified for immediate release. Among them was Chief Motor

Machinist "Bud" Ewers, a 28 year old father from San Francisco. I asked him how he felt and he replied: "Do you remember how you felt on Christmas Eve when you were a little boy?" Chief Forbes who left with him was married and father of a little girl. Both were fortunate to have civilian jobs waiting for them. Forbes had been with the Portland, Oregon fire department before the war and planned to return to the same job. Ross, Ship's Cook First Class, the third one to leave, was returning to San Diego where he and "the Mrs." owned a restaurant.

Time hung heavy on our hands at Subic Bay. Ted Yarger and I hitchhiked up the coast one day, stopping for a beer in the village of Olongapo. It was a miserable place. One long dirt street ran through the center of town. It was lined on both sides with tawdry bars and night clubs, all staffed with "hostesses" prepared to entertain visiting servicemen in upstairs cubbyholes. Most had names like "The All American Bar" or "The Red White and Blue Nite Club". A cacophony of loud off-key jazz could be heard round the clock at most of them. We much preferred the Officers' Club which rambled in tropical splendor through a maze of dense foliage and overlooked the bay. In other villages we observed natives riding carabaos down the street and women balancing huge baskets on their heads. Many of the men wore cast off Army and Navy uniforms and oversized coolie hats. A few drove rickety old cars, but many more drove along in horse driven buggies. The buggies were either two or four seated rigs, built of wood and painted whimsically in orange, green, lavender, and blue. In Manila we saw them used as taxis.

We took the ship down to Manila for a few days and were appalled at the destruction in that once beautiful city. The harbor was strewn with sunken ships, mostly Japanese, and we had to maneuver carefully to avoid them. The city was a shambles. Vic Hampshire, John Bohannon and I went ashore one day and were fortunate to secure a jeep with a competent Filipino driver. After we made our official rounds he drove us through the city. The skyscrapers in the central district were nothing but shells. A Navy office we visited was in a building with bombed out walls but with one elevator still operating. Very few shops were open, but on one of the main streets there were numerous souvenir stands and a few honky tonk night clubs. According to Time Magazine one of these was known as the On-To-Tokyo Bar until the atom bomb was dropped. Then the name changed to The Atom Bomb Bar. When we saw it, it had become the Japanese Surrender Bar.

The heaviest fighting took place on the south side of the city. It was there that the great civic buildings, banks, a music hall, hospitals and other public buildings were located. Many of them were architectural masterpieces spread out among large parks and wide avenues, but none had escaped damage. The Intramuras, the old walled city and the site of the last ditch stand of the Japanese, was nothing but a pile of twisted steel and debris. Farther south was the former American and European residential area of lovely homes and modern apartment buildings. All but one showed the effects of the bombing. Our driver had served in the Philippine Army, been captured and escaped during the infamous "death march". He told us that as the Japanese retreated toward the Intramuras they destroyed each position they had to give up. It was literally house to house fighting with nothing left untouched. England, Belgium, France, Germany, Russia and Japan knew that kind of devastation. The United States was lucky to be spared.

With the Japanese threat behind us we were happy to head north to a cooler climate. The Philippines had been hot and muggy and the duty at Subic Bay was monotonous. Our destination was Okinawa which has a climate not unlike Southern California. After we arrived and replenished our supplies, we learned that it was only a stopover on our way to Korea. In mid September we were on our way as part of a task force to accept the surrender of Japanese naval ships based in Korea. It was a trip fraught with peril because of the mines which had been planted by the Japanese. We proceeded cautiously through the Yellow Sea following minesweepers that cut the mines loose so that they could be exploded. All night long we crept along with searchlights scanning the water to spot unexploded mines. We posted a lookout on the bow but it was Ruffin, our Steward, who was the first to spot a mine. We sank it with our guns, but Ruffin proudly took the honors. There was very little sleep that night. Most of us spent the night on the open decks wearing life jackets. The next morning I sighted what looked like a mine and wheeled the ship out of formation to investigate. It turned out to be a pillow.

The Yellow Sea was well named. Fed by muddy rivers, it is a dark dirty yellow, shallow, choppy and murky. As we approached the southern tip of Korea we could see the island of Saishu To barely visible in the distance. Then we caught sight of Hanna San, a mountain towering over 6000 feet. The temperature dropped to a comfortable 70 degrees which was a welcome and bracing contrast to the hot humid weather we had left behind. We were headed for Inchon, the port city for Seoul a short distance to the east. The Japanese had given each of these cities Japanese names. Inchon became Jinsen and Seoul, the capitol, was called Keijo. It was only a short time before the names reverted back to the original.

Inchon's harbor and anchorage area was surrounded by small islands which gave the impression of a large lake. In early morning the islands were shrouded in a mist. As the sun rose the panoramic scene looked more like a painting on a canvas than a strategic hub of commercial and military activity. It was mid-September and the days were glorious with a bright warm sun and a cool breeze. The harbor was full of sampans, crude flat-botttomed sailboats with smiling Koreans at the helm. They all seemed to be wearing white clothing. Some even had their heads wrapped in white cloth.

Ted Yarger and I went ashore with our first liberty party, setting foot for the first time on continental Asia. The Navy had established a small fleet landing near the Inchon docks and a good part of the native population had assembled to watch the sailors arrive. Near the fleet landing was a large oriental arch painted red, white and blue, bidding a hearty welcome to the Allied forces. In those days Inchon was a city of 60,000 people, but it seemed much smaller. A walk through the streets was a walk back in time. Despite or maybe because of the Japanese occupation there was little evidence of modern innovation. The principal means of transportation was the bicycle. I saw only one automobile, but there were numerous jinrikshas, and a few carts pulled by carabaos. Most of the men shuffled along the streets in wooden sandals, while the women often wore cloth sandals with curling upturned toes. In front of each barber shop was a row of shoes belonging to the customers inside.

Inchon was picturesque from a distance, but the stench from the open sewers was overpowering. After our initial sightseeing tour, I limited my shore visits to official business. On one of these I was walking up a hill to a building which had been taken over by the Navy. On my way I met a middle aged couple who prostrated them-

Ted Yarger and I at the fleet landing in Inchon, Korea, September 21, 1945

Street scenes in Inchon

selves, looking up at me with an imploring gaze. I wasn't sure whether they were Korean or Japanese, probably the latter, but I smiled what I hoped was a smile of reassurance and they continued on their way. On another trip to shore an old man with a flowing white robe stared at me, so I gave him a smile of recognition. He immediately broke into a big smile and bowed several times. He looked distinguished with his well trimmed beard and he carried himself as straight as a telephone pole. Just as friendly was a young man who walked up to me and asked in good English, "Where are you going?" When I didn't answer right away, he smiled, as if to assure me and said "I am Korean."

There were a number of Japanese ships based at Inchon, including a sub-chaser similar to ours and a few weather beaten destroyers. They appeared to be poorly maintained and in need of a good cleaning. After seeing them we wondered how they had been able to inflict so much damage on us. One day we carried the Captain of the battle cruiser, U.S.S. Alaska, and several of his officers on a short trip across the harbor. I told a Commander from the Alaska that I thought I would enjoy duty on his ship because it was so large and stable. He in turn envied the informality and freedom of life aboard a PC.

Philologists would have had a field day with Navy-speak. I hadn't realized how much certain phrases had become part of my everyday language until I read an article in Time Magazine. On the ship we spoke casually of "Adcomphibspac", meaning "Administrative Command of the Amphibious Forces, Pacific". After I had written up the ship's history, Harris, our Yoeman, asked me where to send it. My answer was "Cincpac Pearl". In August I tried to get "Fagairtrans" for a V-12 candidate from our ship who was returning to the States. We were specifying "first available government air transportation." Members of the crew who were eligible for discharge were "separatees."

With no submarines to chase, no amphibious landings to orchestrate, no enemy airplanes to worry about, life on the 804 moved at a much slower pace. At Inchon our duty was reduced to pedestrian chores. At one point we served as an ersatz signpost for a crossroads in the Yellow Sea, directing ships to their ultimate destinations. The weather turned cool with winter winds blowing in from Siberia. To live comfortably on a small ship it is necessary to spread out through the hatches into the fresh air on the open decks. Even then space is limited. With winter approaching we closed the portholes, pulled down the hatches and retreated to our cramped quarters below. In my spare time I read Tolstoy's "War and Peace" and played pinochle. When we tired of pinochle I suggested that we try contract bridge, a game none of us knew how to play. Our library included a copy of Hoyle, so it became our bible for the night. With every move we referred to the rules, arguing about interpretation, and eating peanuts. It took us from 6:00 P.M. to 1:00 A.M. to finish three rubbers, but we had a wonderful time.

Just when we began to dispair of going south to a warmer clime, we had good news. Our base of operations was shifting to Shanghai, China. My impressions of Shanghai had come almost exclusively from Charlie Chan movies. I pictured it as a city of excitement and mystery and I wasn't disappointed. Buoyed with anticipation we souped up our diesel engines and set a course for the mouth of the Yangtze River.

Paris Of The East

The Paris of the East, it was called. Cosmopolitan, bustling, exotic, mysterious, Shanghai was a cultural crossroads and the quintessential liberty town for sailors. Enroute from Inchon the crew was getting ready. Shoes were shined, beards were trimmed and dress uniforms were laundered. We had the luxury of an English pilot to guide us through the multi-pronged channels of the Yangtze River delta. We listened carefully and observed as he maneuvered us through the twists and turns of the mighty river. After the initial trip we would be on our own as we sailed in and out of Shanghai. Moving inland from the Yellow Sea we reached the mouth of the Huang Pu, Shanghai's river which empties into the Yangtze. The Huang Pu is deep and turbulent with a swift flowing current which approaches seven knots. It presents a challenge to the most experienced navigator, not only because of the current but because of the traffic. Sampans, barges, junks, water taxis, ferry boats, and ships of every description criss-cross the channel with little regard to the International Rules of The Road. To thread our way up the Huang Pu we switched to a Danish pilot who, after twenty five years on the job, knew every eddy of the treacherous river.

As we approached the city we were surprised to see Japanese soldiers, with rifles, walking or lounging on a wall along the riverbank. They posed no threat, but had yet to be interned. The river became more congested as we neared the city. Hundreds of sampans and junks, some with colorful sails unfurled, darted across our path or skimmed along with us. The larger boats flew large Chinese flags and pennants to denote the organizations to which they belonged. The Chinese have a superstition that a boat must have eyes to see where it is going, so each one has a large eye on each side of the bow. Junks built in Foochow have a flared open bow, and with two eyes, look like monsters coming down the stream.

The 804 docked just north of Soochow Creek, not far from Shanghai's famous Bund, the banking and commercial center of the International Settlement. Its magnificent buildings, reflecting the architecture of 19th century Europe, lined the waterfront and gave the impression of colonial power and influence. Not far away were the pagodas and oriental rooftops rising from the Chinese sector of

A PC moored next to the cruiser Nashville, with Shanghai skyline in the background.

the city. Our arrival was a big event for the opportunistic Chinese who descended like a swarm of locusts, eager to benefit from the American largess. I described the scene in a letter:

"Hundreds of native boats, with everything to sell, swarmed alongside and hung onto the ship with large hooks. We yelled at them to go away but they only smiled and bowed. All day yesterday and today they have continued to cluster around. I learned that "chee", spoken with a snarl, means 'go away' and works temporarily. But the most effective way to keep them off is the fire hose. We have it rigged aft now and shower the boats when they get too close. They are unauthorized merchants, selling everything from suitcases to women, so we don't like to have them around."

"At the same time that the leeches closed in from the river a parade of Chinese businessmen arrived on the dock and presented their credentials. Mr. W. Ching offered his services as our laundryman and cleaning and pressing specialist. We accepted so he and his helper moved aboard. The helper set up his pressing equipment on deck and Mr. Ching began to collect our laundry. A few minutes later, Mr. Ha Ching arrived and presented credentials showing that he was a reliable tailor. He moved aboard with his helpers and a Singer sewing machine and started work amidships. After wearing unpressed khaki and tattle-tale grey underclothes for months, it is a luxurious feeling to be well dressed again. We turned down one outfit that wanted to scrape and chip paint for 85 cents a day, but we did engage Mr. Yung Chew, a very good barber, who has a spot back on the fantail. Probably as a token of good will, he cut my hair today for 'no charge'."

"These men consider that they are working for us exclusively. They arrive every morning at about 0800 and stay until 1700. When they arrive they stick their heads in the

W. CHING		
LAUNDRY WORKING SHPI'S		
U. S. S.		193
NAME		
MARK	DATE	
吊 被	Hommnack	$. 50
占 條	Blankte	$. 50
粗 代	Sae bay	$. 30
占 水 衫	Jumpers. Blue,	$. 30
占 水 庫	Trouesrs. Blue	$. 30
藍 長 庫	Trouesrs. Dungaree	
藍 汗 衫	Shirts Dungaree	
被 旦	Sheet.	
被 套	Mattrers. Covers.	
檯 布	Toblecloth	
藍令水衫	Jumpers. Dress	
白 水 衫	Jumpers undress	
白 大 衣	Uniformcoats. White	
白 水 庫	Uniform Trouesrs. White	
中 衫	Jackets. Mess	
毛 巾	Towels. Bath	
面 布	Towels. Face	
枕 套	Pillow Case	
汗 衫	Shirts White	
綢 汗 衫	Shirts Silk	
連 衫 庫	Union Shrits	
襪 衫	Undshirts	
小 庫	Drawers	
反 旦	Aprons	
茶 布	Napken	
脚 布	Leggins. Pair	
白 帽	Hat. Whits	
帽 套	Caps. Cove	
黑 襪	Sock Black	
黑 絲 襪	Sock Black Silk	
小 襪	Sock White	
絲 襪	Sock Silk	
占 襪	Sock Wallon	
白 巾	Hondker Chiefs	
庫 帶	Belt	
令 子	Collors	
衣 代	Laundry Bay	
Total	Pieces.	

Mr. Ching's laundry list, customized for Navy personnel

wardroom door, salute and say 'good morning, officers'. At night they salute again and say 'I go now'. They resent any infringement on their monopoly. This morning, at Mr. Ching's request, I chased off a pressing man who had slipped aboard and set up a rival pressing shop without our knowledge. I also chased off a Chinese dentist who was selling false teeth and a Chinese mess boy who had 'occupied' the mess hall with nobody's permission and was washing the dishes."

Our first shore excursion lived up to all we had heard about the wonders of Shanghai. Once ashore Vic Hampshire, Hal Bodenstab, and I walked to the gate on Yangtzepoo Road and were besieged by ricksha and pedicab drivers. We opted for a pedicab, a two wheeled cart rigged to the front part of a bicycle. It was a common form of transportation, rapidly replacing rickshas which were pulled by haggard hunger-driven coolies on foot. To ride in a pedicab, particularly downhill, was a thrilling experience. We bounced along, tearing in and out through crowds of pedestrians, other pedicabs, rickshas, streetcars and a few automobiles. The streets were narrow and packed with throngs of jabbering people of every nationality. The shops were filled with a fascinating array of items from all over the world. Flags, lanterns, and colorful banners hung above the entrances.

Shanghai had its Fifth Avenue on Nanking Road which was lined with skyscrapers, modern hotels, department stores and swank shops. It cut through the center of the International Settlement and

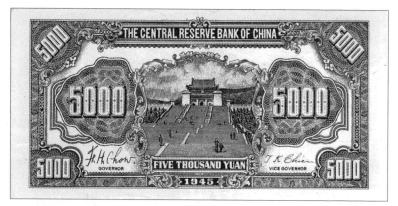

A 5000 Yuan note of the official Chinese National Currency, worth about five U.S. dollars.

continued into the posh residential area where many embassies and the mansions of wealthy Chinese were located. When we first arrived, silk robes, camphor chests, jade jewelry, and Chinese porcelain could be purchased at a fraction of what they would have cost in the United States. Inflation and the influx of American servicemen put pressure on prices which began to spiral upward and by late November were scandalously high. Servicemen began to boycott stores and restaurants and military authorities put the Park Hotel and a number of other establishments out of bounds because of price gouging. Finally General Wedemeyer issued a public statement demanding a sweeping investigation of prices.

Whether paying the tab in restaurants or buying gifts, a dual currency system was a constant source of confusion. After the Japanese surrender the Central Reserve Bank of China had issued a new national currency(C.N.C.) at an exchange rate of roughly 1000 yuan to one dollar. During the occupation the Japanese puppet government had issued a Reserve Currency which was still in circulation at a rate of over 100,000 yuan to the dollar. Most merchants had switched to the new Chinese currency but there were still some who would accept only the former. As a result our pockets were stuffed with the bills of both currencies. With the value of the currencies fluctuating from day to day, we needed more than an abacus to translate yuan into dollars. On the 18th of October I went to the bank and bought C.N.C. yuan at a rate of 800 to the dollar. The

Menu from one of several fine restaurants in Shanghai's Park Hotel

same day I bought some Reserve Currency yuan at the rate of 184,000 to the dollar.

In marked contrast to the International Settlement was the Chinese sector of the city, a sprawling mass of humanity, alive with the cacophony of a language we didn't understand and the pungent odors of oriental cooking. Chinese restaurants abounded and many served food which was acceptable to Western palates. We passed a palatial tea house which was a well known landmark. There was an elegance about the place except for a pile of stones to the left of the front foor which served as a urinal for men in a hurry. I'm not sure what the women did. Wending our way through the crowded streets was difficult because of the street peddlars, flower girls, and beggars who clung to us. We were able to shake them off with the help of the police who often intervened. The traffic cops in Shanghai were a colorful breed. Most were tall, turbaned, bearded Hindus.

After my first foray into the Chinese sector I paid a memorable return visit with a former APc skipper, "Mac" McGraw. "Mac" and his wife Frances had become my good friends during our stint at the refresher training school in Miami. "Mac" surfaced in Shanghai aboard another PC and got in touch with me. One Sunday afternoon

he asked me to join him and two other officers from his ship on a tour of Shanghai. Our guide was going to be Albert Ya, the 22 year old son of Ah Kong, "Mac's" tailor. When he heard what was planned, Vic Hampshire also joined the group. We rode in rickshas all the way and Albert insisted on paying the fares. He said it was "out of friendship for his noble friends." It also prevented haggling over the price.

Albert took us to parts of the old Chinese city we would never have discovered by ourselves. The streets were the

Mac McGraw and I when we were both operating on APc's in the Solomons.

narrowest we had seen, but jammed with thousands of people from all stratas of Chinese society. Well dressed businessmen rubbed shoulders with beggars in rags. Sore-ridden children clung to us asking for money. Coolies with calloused bare feet trotted along pulling rickshas over the cobblestone streets, but they didn't have to contend with automobiles. There were none. Nor were there sidewalks, so the crowds surged in and out of the shops and into the streets. There were open sewers and foul smells. The shops sold chopsticks and firecrackers and just about everything else, much of which we would label as junk. Firecrackers were likely to go off at any time anywhere, which some times made us feel that we were in a war zone. To cut down on the noise the city had passed an ordinance that no firecrackers could be lighted after 7:00 P.M.

Albert took us to a large Buddhist temple. There on the first floor was a place of worship in the presence of an enormous Buddha. On the second floor were many different Buddhas, representing the torments of the hereafter for various sins of the living. On the third floor were the age Buddhas, one for each year of a person's life. As we left the temple we watched a procession honoring Buddha. An image of Buddha was carried in a sedan chair by four priests while other priests in silk robes and masks walked solemnly alongside. Albert paid us a compliment by inviting us to his home for dinner. We thought it wise to decline in view of warnings the Navy had given us about dysentery, but we agreed to go to his home. When we arrived he followed the ceremonial tradition of indicating chairs and serving

A war correspondent describes his trip on a sister ship of the PC-804 and how happy he was to reach dry land.

tea. His mother made the tea and poured while Albert, who spoke fluent English, steered us through the conversational difficulties.

Shanghai wasn't one big holiday as it might appear. The business of managing the ship continued and there were routine trips down the Huang Pu and Yangzte into the Yellow Sea. Floating mines were a hazard to ocean shipping, so the 804 served as an escort for the large troop ships and merchant vessels traveling in and out of Shanghai. Our job was to lead ships through the coastal waters, keeping on the alert for any mines which lay ahead. On one of its assignments the 804 escorted the S.S. Adabelle Lykes, filled with home-bound G.I.'s, as far as the East China Sea. Another time on a dark night we were escorting a hospital ship through the islands near the mouth of the Yangtze when our spotlight focused on a mine almost dead ahead. We flashed a pre-arranged emergency signal to the hospital ship to make a sharp turn to port. After a few moments they sent back a message which read "do not understand your signal". We held our breath, expecting to see a big explosion, but luck was with them and they missed the mine, by how much we could only guess.

On November 3rd Vic Hampshire received orders transferring him to a new assignment as skipper of a PCE, a smaller version of a destroyer escort. At the same time orders came for me to take command of the 804. The change of command took place later in the month. It was a good feeling to take command after serving so long in the number two position. I expressed my satisfaction in a letter: "I am getting some darned good experience in the Navy. The responsibility of organizing and managing a multi-million dollar ship, with its problems of supply, personnel, maintenance, power, etc., is no mean job. And with the Navy setup, I run the show. No board of directors, except the distant rules, regulations, and general policies issued by the Department of the Navy." The Navy learned long ago how to delegate. There was a command hierarchy but aboard ship the commanding officer's word was law.

With Vic Hampshire's departure a new replacement arrived to bring our officer staff up to complement. He was a twenty year old Ensign from North Carolina named Robin (Bob) Kirby. To my surprise another neophyte, Ensign Webster Smith, no older than Robin and fresh from the States, arrived an hour after I was sworn in as Captain. He had orders attaching him to the 804, putting us over our normal complement of officers. Both he and Robin came to us directly from the Navy's V-12 training program. The Navy seemed to be making an effort to season some of its most junior officers as more and more of its experienced officers became eligible for discharge. Shortly after Kirby and Smith arrived, John Bohannon and his communications control team were transferred to Pearl Harbor. With the war over, the functions they performed were no longer needed. As pros they had been a great help in the communications department. Soon Ted Yarger was also on his way home.

In subsequent weeks I had to scramble to recruit the number of men we needed to replace those who were ready for discharge. As soon as they were eligible, the men were anxious to get home. Harry C. Lloyd, our very able signalman, was one of them. Age 24, he owned a grocery store in Emporium, Pennsylvania. His mother had been running it in his absence and he wanted to get back to relieve her of the responsibility. The rapid turnover was a problem. No sooner did we get replacements than the replacements themselves became eligible for discharge. We reached a point where only a third of the original crew were on board.

Shanghai was a city of contrasts and nowhere was it more apparent than in the disparity between rich and poor. A young woman with a small child, pushing the oar of a sampan against the strong current, hovered close to the stern of our ship whenever we were in port. When she tried to tie up to the ship, our crew, following Navy regulations, forced her to back away. She was there for only one reason, to salvage what she could from the garbage we threw overboard. It was the only way she and the child could survive. Not long after he joined us, Web Smith was standing a watch while we were in port. He called to me from the flying bridge with a hint of urgency in his voice. When I got there he pointed to a corpse, a fully dressed Chinese male, floating down the river. Web assumed we should notify the port authorities, but I assured him that was not necessary. "Nothing to be alarmed about" I told him. "It happens every day." I could tell that Web was shocked and I'm sure he wondered about my apparent callousness.

The "haves" among the Chinese were equally visible. Two brothers who owned the swank Park Hotel on Nanking Road were graduates of the University of Southern California. One afternoon they hosted a party for USC graduates who were based with the Armed Forces in Shanghai. Two of our officers were USC alums, so they rendezvoused at the Park and were whisked by limousine to a magnificent country estate where they were served an elaborate buffet dinner. The foreigners in the International Settlement also lived well. Many were American and European business executives and there was a large corps of consular officials who drove around town in chauffer driven automobiles.

Night life in Shanghai was dazzling to the eyes of young Navy officers who had been living a Spartan life for the past several years. On our first shore excursion, Vic Hampshire, Hal Bodenstab and I joined a friend from another ship to tour the French Quarter. We first stopped at a bar, well known to Navy personnel, where Vic hired a beautiful Russian girl to accompany us for the evening. The five of us then set out for Arcadia, a lavish Russian night club in the French quarter. Arcadia occupied a large modern building designed as a night club with a magnificent foyer, court yards, alcoves, private dining rooms and a tiered central dining area where a twelve piece orchestra played classical music during dinner and music for dancing after dinner. It seemed to be a congregating place for the beautiful people of Shanghai. The floor show featured Russian singers and dancers.

Shanghai had become a haven for the Russian gentry who fled their country after the Tzar was overthrown. Lala, the girl Vic brought along on our night club outing, was a second generation product of the exodus. Her family settled first in Manchuria and later moved to Shanghai. Not only was she beautiful, but she was intelligent, well read and well informed. As she and Vic developed a strong attachment to each other, she became a helpful resource, briefing us on the local history and culture, steering us to the best shops and restaurants, and brightening up what otherwise could have been all male social occasions.

Lala came from that strata of society known as the demi-monde. Women of similar background were often seen at the Officers Club atop the Sun-Sun Building in downtown Shanghai. During the Japanese occupation the same club played host to Japanese officers. One night a bartender at the club told me: "Not much has changed. Only the uniforms. The women are all the same." Somewhat lower

Officers of the PC-804 dining at the Officer's Club atop the Sun Sun Building in downtown Shanghai. From left to right: Bob Kirby, Web Smith, Vic Hampshire, Jim Schultz, Ted Yarger, and Hal Bodenstab.

on the social scale were the dance hall hostesses. Bob MacDowell and I dropped in one evening at the Paramount Ballroom where we paid the equivalent of $2 an hour to dance with two attractive Chinese girls. They explained in English that they were university students who were helping out because of the influx of American servicemen. Whether or not that was true, we thought they were charming and we had a good time. Farther down the social ladder were the bar girls and there were thousands of them in Shanghai. They hustled drinks for the house and socialized with the customers, but were not supposed to date them. That rule was often broken with a whispered word to the bartender and a little cash. At the bottom rung were the brothels and they abounded in Shanghai.

Fraternization with prostitutes sometimes created problems for the Navy. One day our top rated radioman came to me and asked permission to be married. As skipper I had to give my approval before a wedding could take place. I asked him to tell me about his intended bride. She was Chinese. He had met her in a bar and was convinced he was in love. I suggested that he invite her to have Sunday dinner on the ship so that I could meet her. He agreed and brought her aboard a week later. I had seen some cute Chinese girls, but I wasn't prepared for the two ugly women who paraded up the gangplank that Sunday noon. His friend had brought her girlfriend. Both were dressed in full length mink coats and their smiles revealed an ample number of gold teeth. I couldn't imagine this fine looking young man from Kansas returning home with one of these girls in tow. I could have said an emphatic 'no', but I wanted him to make the decision. After the women left I had several heart to heart talks with him, but it was only after I brought up the issue of children that he reluctantly decided it would not be a good idea.

Two incidents on the Huang Pu underscored how dangerous the river could be. One day I went by motor launch to a meeting aboard the cruiser St. Paul which was moored in the middle of the river. The St. Paul at that time was the command ship for the Seventh Fleet of which the 804 was a part. I had just left the meeting and was about to signal my launch when General Quarters was sounded aboard the ship. Immediately bells began to ring, whistles blew and crew members were running in all directions. I flattened myself against a bulkhead to keep out of the way. Then there was a bang and a shudder

It was front page news when a Japanese LST, out of control on the Huang Pu River, rammed the U.S. cruiser St. Paul, as pictured.

as a Japanese LST, out of control, slammed into the St. Paul ripping open a big hole in the bow. It was a couple of hours before things calmed down and I was able to leave the ship.

On another occasion I was conning the 804 down the Huang Pu when a makeshift flat- bottomed barge started across the river directly in our path. The barge was piled high with bags of flour. I signaled with the customary two blasts of our whistle for both of us to turn right which would have avoided a collision. The barge did not respond and probably had no idea what the signal meant. Meanwhile, it kept coming on a zigzag course until it seemed inevitable that we were going to collide. I backed our engines full speed until we almost came to a stop, but there was still enough forward movement for our bow to nudge gently into the sacks of flour. It was enough to send clouds of flour flying into the air. The Chinese bargemen screamed and shouted what were probably obscenities, but when the air cleared we could see that there was no serious damage. I continued on, hoping that we hadn't created an international incident.

I continued to run into old friends, some from the Navy and some from Allegheny and Meadville. Don Leberman, with whom I had gone to high school, turned up in Shanghai after spending a year and a half with Chinese guerrillas who were fighting the Japanese invaders. Don was serving with a U.S. intelligence unit which had been flown in from Burma and dropped by parachute into enemy territory. He operated a clandestine radio to transmit reports on the weather and troop movements, moving from place to place to avoid detection. When the war was over he travelled by sampan for several days to reach Shanghai. Don knew his way around China and introduced us to many of the sights of Shanghai that we had not seen. He also steered us to Sun Ya, a Cantonese restaurant where we learned to use chopsticks and had the best Chinese food we had ever tasted.

In December it turned cold. There was a coal shortage in Shanghai and even the elegant Cathay Hotel could not keep its rooms heated. In blustery weather we sailed down the Yangtze to rendezvous with an aircraft carrier in the East China Sea and guide it up the river to Shanghai. It required some tricky navigation and the staff office asked me in advance if I thought I could handle it. I assured them I

MISCELLANEOUS DISHES 雜類菜

Small order for party of 2 to 4 persons

Order No.		Price
86.	Beef Curry	
87.	Beef with Oyster Sauce	
90.	Beef with Vegetable	
91.	Beef with Onion	
96.	Beef with Bamboo Shoots	
100.	Sweet and Sour Pork* (boneless)	
101.	Sweet and Sour Pork Ribs	
102.	Shredded Pork with Vegetable	
103.	Shredded Pork with Salted Parsnips**	
104.	Shredded Pork with Green Pepper	
107.	Braised Pork with Bamboo Shoots**	
108.	Sliced Pork, Fried with flour coating	
109.	Sliced Roast Pork with Vegetable	
154.	Fresh Mushrooms, Pan-broiled	
155.	Vegetarian's Dish De Luxe	
156.	Fresh Mushrooms with Bamboo Shoots	
157.	Bamboo Shoots with Dried Mushrooms	
159.	The Vegetarian's Dish	
160.	Bean Sprouts—Plain Sauté	
161.	Vegetable with Cream Sauce	
163.	Soya Bean Curd with Mushrooms	
165.	Plain Green Vegetable in season	
166.	Bamboo Shoots with Brown Sauce***	Variable

(Continued on next page)

*A very popular Cantonese dish among foreigners.
**Home style dishes which go very well with plain rice.
***This dish is best in Winter and Spring. Not recommended in Summer.

— 3 —

MISCELLANEOUS DISHES—Continued

Order No.		Price
167.	Shrimp Curry	$
168.	Shrimps—Plain Sauté	
169.	Shrimps with Green Peas	
170.	Shrimp and Potato Salad	
171.	Fried Shrimp Balls	
172.	Shrimps with Scrambled Eggs	
173.	Diced Kidney with Shrimps etc.	
174.	Prawn in Sections, Brown Sauce	variable
175.	Prawn in Sections, Pan-broiled	" "
176.	Fried Prawn Meat	
177.	Sliced Prawn Meat Sauté	" "
178.	Layer Prawns with Ham	" "
180.	Chop Suey	
181.	Omelet with Bamboo Shoots etc.	
183.	Fried Giblets (without flour coating)	
184.	Chicken Liver with Bamboo Shoots	
185.	Fried Chicken Liver	
186.	Fried Chicken Liver with Ham	
203.	Minced Meat with Fried Bean Curd	

— 4 —

The Sun Ya restaurant was reputed to have the best Chinese food in Shanghai. After eating there, I had to agree.

could, but I was relieved when we found the carrier and made our way back to Shanghai with no problems. We had ice on the decks from the freezing temperature, but the Navy issue fur-lined coats and hoods kept us warm. We spotted a mine on the return trip and Bob MacDowell who served as Gunnery Officer exploded it with a machine gun. Some weeks later a Japanese repatriation ship, the Enoshima Maru, was not so lucky. It struck a mine in the same location with a loss of 110 passengers.

We did the best we could to make Christmas a festive affair. Ruffin, our steward, was missing that morning. In checking around we learned that he had been in a fight while on liberty and was being held by the Shore Patrol. Web Smith with the help of one of the mess cooks stepped in to help with the Christmas dinner preparations. He made hors d'oevres and spiced tomato juice which he served in silver goblets which Bob Kirby had bought from a street vendor. He paid $11 for the goblets but Mr. Ching said they were nothing but copper and not worth it. A small Christmas tree was the centerpiece and our dinner featured roast turkey, baked ham, sage stuffing, mashed potatoes, giblet gravy, creamed peas, apple pie, fruit cake, plum pudding with brandy sauce, mixed nuts and coffee. The credit for such a good meal went to Chief Cook Hughes.

We ushered in the New Year with no fanfare, anchored at the mouth of the Yangtze. We had been dispatched to spend a week there as a pilot vessel. It was a dismal assignment and we were happy to return to the bright lights of Shanghai. Within a few days we received the good news that at long last we were scheduled to return to the United States. For reasons of experience and seniority, I was put in charge of a four ship flotilla destined for decommissioning in San Diego. All were PC Class vessels. The crew pitched in with more than their usual enthusiasm to prepare for what would be a long journey. But this time they would be headed for home. Two of the ships had engine problems which could not be remedied in Shanghai, so it was going to be slow-going.

It was a red letter day when we sailed down the Huang Pu for the last time. Our signalman had made a 'homeward bound' pennant, 56 feet long, which streamed from the mast. There were five white stars, one for each officer, on a blue field, with one foot of red and white bunting for each member of the crew. As part of the special communications equipment which had been put on board for amphibious landings, there was a large bull horn which could be heard for two to three miles. We had never put it to use except in practice exercises, but we decided the time had come to put it to the test. We looked through our supply of phonograph records and decided that Jo Stafford's rendition of "The Long Way Home" was the most appropriate. We picked two other selections, "Sentimental Journey" and "California Here I Come" to include in our repertoire and played them through the bull horn as we sailed down the river. I'm sure that half of Shanghai could have heard our musical message. As we passed the cruiser Los Angeles it signaled "goodbye and good sailing."

I checked with Fleet Weather Central the night before we left and was assured that we would have clear weather. That was when I learned you could never trust a weatherman. (That doesn't apply to weather women — I married one). As we moved from the Yangtze into the Yellow Sea we ran into a strong north wind which was blowing up heavy seas and obscuring visibility. Enormous swells were tossing the ship from one side to the other. At one point our senior radioman was thrown against a bulkhead, sustaining a deep gash across the top of his head. We had been ordered to leave the only medical person we had on board, a Chief Pharmacist's Mate, in Shanghai, so we had no one qualified to give him the attention he should have had. I was called and did what I could, shaving and cleansing his scalp and sprinkling sulfa powder into the wound.

The radioman wasn't our only casualty on the trip. Harris, our capable Yeoman, had been hospitalized in Shanghai with a nervous disorder, but had returned to the ship with a clean bill of health. Shortly after we left Shanghai, he had a relapse and spent most of the time in his bunk, completely out of touch with reality. Another problem occurred when a blister in the palm of the hand of one of the seamen became infected. When the infection began to spread into his arm we became alarmed, so I sterilized the area and lanced the swollen part with a surgical knife. That seemed to get the infection under control, but I was anxious to get my three patients into a hospital for professional care. I sent a radio dispatch to Guam, the first stop on our homeward bound trip, and asked them to have a hospital launch meet our ship on arrival. Then I reached the skippers of the other three ships and asked them if they thought they could get to Guam on their own. We were only two days away at that point. They answered in the affirmative so I revved up the engines and proceeded to Guam at flank speed.

The run from Shanghai to Guam had been harrowing. Not only were there medical problems and rough seas, but three of the crew had gone wild on the last day of liberty in Shanghai. They raised enough hell to catch the attention of Naval authorities. I took them into my custody so that we could leave on schedule. After we were underway I held a Captain's Mast and awarded each of them a deck court martial.

It was a relief to arrive in Guam and deliver my three patients into professional hands. A day later I was able relax even more when I saw the other three ships make their way into the harbor. After a few days in Guam we left for Eniwetok, a desolate atoll in the Marshall Islands, where we we stayed overnight for refueling. We had rough seas all the way from Guam and half the crew was seasick. The ship would rise on the crest of a huge wave, then plunge down through the next wave with such force that water poured across the bow. Meanwhile the whole ship vibrated as if it would fall to pieces. After we crossed the International Dateline we had a couple of days of calm weather, but then we ran into a "kona" storm which lasted until we were a day out of Oahu. Having finally arrived in Pearl Harbor I arranged for Hal Bodenstab to succeed me as Captain, a job for which he had been groomed from the time that Vic Hampshire left the ship. Hal was an Engineering Officer and not an officer of the line, but on a ship the size of a PC every officer became a Jack-of-all-trades and we both knew he could handle it. The change of command took place on February 13, 1946. Ensigns Smith and Kirby had developed into first rate officers so the ship was in good hands as it sailed to San Diego for decommissioning.

Two days later I boarded a Navy cargo ship, the U.S.S. Alamance (AKA-75) as a passenger and headed for San Francisco. I shared a spacious cabin with the only other passenger, another Navy Lieutenent. We soon discovered that a well stocked pantry separated us from the Captain's quarters so we foraged for late afternoon snacks at cocktail time. By the time we passed under the Golden Gate bridge five days later we were well fed and well rested. I reported to the Officers' Separation Center in San Francisco for processing to inactive status in the Naval Reserve and my Navy saga came to an end.. Two months later the 804 passed into history. On April 18 I received a Western Union telegram from Web Smith. It read: "Eight Zero Four Out Of Commission With Flying Colors." It was a ship which had served us well.

UNITED STATES NAVY

28 FEB....
SAN PEDRO, CAL.

DEAR JIM,
            GREETINGS AND WELCOME BACK TO CIVILIAN
LIFE. HOW DOES IT FEEL ? WE AT LEAST KNOW THAT
YOU ARE BACK IN THE STATES AS MY VAL-PAC WAS HOME
WHEN WE ARRIVED HERE.
            NOW FOR A BRIEF SUMMARY OF THE LAST LEG
OF THE TRIP. WE LEFT ON THURSDAY JUST A LITTLE
WHILE AFTER YOU LEFT. IT WAS A GOOD TRIP ALL THE
WAY... WE MADE STANDARD DOWN TEN MOST OF THE WAY.
ARRIVING IN S.D. THE FOLLOWING FRIDAY MORNING. WE
SLOWED DOWN DURING THE LAST DAY TO MADE A DAYLITE
ARRIVAL. WE RAN INTO HEAVY FOG JUST OFF THE
ENTRANCE BUOY.. SO WE JUST WAITED UNTIL NOON.
WE HAD ORDERS THE DAY BEFORE ARRIVING TO HAVE OUR
ELIGBLE MEN READY FOR TRANSFER UPON ARRIVAL.
WE PULLED INTO THE DOCKS, AND TRANSFERED 14 MEN
OFF WITHIN 15 MINUTES. WE HELD CORBETT AND SYLVESTER
FROM FRIDAY UNTIL WEDNESDAY WE WERE MOORED IN THE
BAY WITH EXCELLENT BOAT SERVICE.... WE WERE DIRECTED
TO COME HERE FOR FURTHER DISPOSAL. SO WEDNESDAY
MORNING WE CAME UP HERE... FLANK SPEED ALL THE WAY
UP... FOGGY TOO. WE WERE SET OUT TOWARD CATALINA
BUT TOOK RADAR CUTS AND USED THE FATHOMETER AND
WE CAME RIGHT UP TO THE BREAKWATER WITH NO STRAIN.
            WE ARE MOORED OFF TERMINAL ISLAND (NOT
IN THE CHANNEL. WITH THE 807, 801 AND 802.....
THEY HAVE BEEN HERE ALMOST A MONTH AND NOTHING
HAPPENS. THE ONLY TROUBLE YOU CAN'T GET REPLACEMENTS.
THE 801 HAS ONLY TWO OFFICERS.... WE HAVE SECURED
THE WARDROOM PANTRY AND EAT IN THE MESS HALL.
THE 804 IS TO BE DECOMMISSIONED AS A VESSEL FOR
SALE, SO THE ENGINES ARE NOT COMING OUT AND WE
ARE GOING TO START PRESERVING THE HULL (THE 804
IS NOT GOING TO BE IN THE RESERVE FLEET. IT'S
ONLY THE SECOND DAY HERE SO HALL AND MAC AND STILL
IN THE PROCESS OF REPORTING IN... ETC. THE SHIP
IS TO BE PAINTED HAZE GREY AND IN A FEW WEEKS WE
WILL BE IN WONDERFUL SHAPE. THE MEN WE PICKED UP
AT PEARL ARE ALL GOOD MEN AND WILLING WORKERS.

U. S. NAVAL OPERATING BASE
Terminal Island (San Pedro)
California

18 March 1946

Dear Jim,

I received your letter yesterday and was mighty glad to hear from you. And I imagine by this time you are all fit out in those civilian clothes.

I suppose that you were happy to be separated out here instead of having to go all the way to NEW YORK and then back track to Meadville. How did you find everything at home—bet you haven't had a quiet minute to yourself. Say what did they say about that pot belly of yours.

In your letter you mentioned some rough weather between Pearl and Frisco - I guess that we were to far South or to far ahead to get any of it,much to my pleasure. Our ship arrived on the west coast the 22nd,about forty hours ahead of schelude. Although most of the fellows stayed up all night to get the first glimpse of the states,it turned out so foggy that morning that it was nearly ten o'clock before we could go on ih the harbor.

While in San Diego,we all looked up Bohannon and had quite a week-end there. By the way Bo got his leave but didn't get married. I guess that will come later. After a few days there,we were sent on up to San Pedro for disposal by ComEleven. Our ship was moored at the PC nest alongside the 801,802,807,&1144 in the inner mole just alittle way fro the Administration Building at Roosevelt Base. The PC-810 has already been decommissioned,and she is certainly a bare ship. There is an awful lot of paper work and inventories along with the preservation of the ship. Oub date for decommisssioning has been set as the 16th of April but believe that it will be closer to the end of the month.

Last week our ship was made Mother Ship for the PC nest which sounds natural for us. However,today the 801,802,804,and 807 was moved alongside the LST 969 which is assuming the Mother duty. Personnel has been moving on and off regularly,although we haven't been able to get a Stewart Mate or anyone for us officers, Consequently we have been eating down in the mess hall. Say tthanks alot for that money order—we all had decided to chip in to cover the loss instead of trying to slip it through. I am certainly sorry that it happened that way in the first place.

I have talked to Helen several times,and I am trying to get an annulment here in California—as I have already filed and waiting for court date. Otherwise,I could have gotten orders back to New York for duty until my time was up. Hope to get separated out here so that I can go directly to Ohio,in which case I'LL probably drive through PA and will try to get up to see you.

YOUR OLD PAL

Mac

After I left the 804, Web Smith and Bob MacDowell continued to keep me informed.

PS : AM SET FOR THE COLLEGE OF EDUCATION THIS FALL.. AT USC

U. S. S. LSM-348
C/O FLEET POST OFFICE
SAN FRANCISCO, CALIFORNIA

SAN DIEGO: 10 May, 1946

DEAR JIM:

      WELL BOTH OF YOUR JUNIOR OFFICERS REALLY STEPPED INTO
THE BIGTIME. BOTH BOB AND I HAVE COMMAND OF ONE OF THESE GREEN
DRAGONS. BUT FIRST LET ME CATCH UP WITH THE PAST ....
      THE 804 WENT INTO DRYDOCK OR RATHER, ALONGSIDE THE DOCK
AROUND THE TENTH OF APRIL. IT WAS A MAD WEEK OF TEARING UP THE
SHIP. THE READY BOXES, GUNS AND MOUNTS,AND DEPTH CHARGE EQUIPMENT
ALL CAME OFF, ALSO THE ELECTRONIC GEAR... THE SHIP WAS THEN COVERED
FROM STEM TO STERN WITH A PRESERVATIVE " CONSOL OIL " AND DIFFERENT
GRADES WERE USED ON THE ENGINES... WAX ON THE GALLEY GEAR...ETC
WE CHECKED OUT OF SUPPLY IN FINE SHAPE TOO... YOU HAVE NO IDEA
OF ALL THE THINGS WE FOUND THAT WE COULDN'T FIND WHEN WE NEED--
ED THEM... EVERYTHING FROM YEAR OLD CHEESE SANDWICHES TO HEAVEN
ONLY KNOWS WHAT....THE ACTUAL CEREMONY CAUGHT US BY SUPPRISE.
IT WAS SUPPOSED TO GO OFF AT 5 PM BUT THEY CAME AROUND ABOUT NOON ,
WE ALL LINEDUP IN VARIOUS STAGES OF DRESS THEY BLEW A WHISTLE
SHOOK HANDS WITH HAL AND WENT TO THE NEXT SHIP... WE STILL HAD
THE CREWS TRANSFER PAPERS, AND FINAL SHIPS RECORDS.. PLUS THE
TYPEWRITERS TO GET RID OF..
      WE REALLY THREW A PARTY THAT NITE... THE OFFICERS OF THE
807, 04, 02 and 01. REALLY WENT WILD...
      HAL IS ON A 35 DAY LEAVE AND WILL REPORT TO NY , MAC WAS
SEPARATED, AND WENT EAST TO CLEVELAND, AND WAS GOING TO SEE YOU
IF POSSIBLE. BOB AND I LOAFED AROUND ROOSEVELT BASE FOR A WEEK
OR SO AND THEN GOT THESE ASSIGNMENTS. HE IS ON THE LSM # 350.
THIS SHIP WAS OVER IN CERRITOS CHANNEL WHEN I TOOK COMMAND, IV'E
TWO OTHER ENSIGNS JUNIOR TO MYSELF IN AGE AND SEA DUTY(IF YOU
CAN IMAGINE THAT) AND A CREW OF THIRTY NINE MEN. THE SHIP IS
TO RETURN TO CHINA SOMETIME THIS SUMMER WITH A COMPLETE USN CREW.
IT IS JUST A MATTER OF TIME WAITING FOR A RELIEF, BUT I MAY STAY
ON DURING THE SUMMER IF THE SHIP DOES NOT LEAVE THE STATES. I'VE
NO YEOMAN, SO AM HAVING A GREAT TIME KEEPING UP WITH REPORTS.
SHIPS SERVICE, COMMISSARY, AND TITLE B ARE IN GOOD SHAPE, THE
REASON: THE SHIP CARRIED THE STAFF... SO THE COMBINATION WARD-
ROOM AND BERTHING SPACE IS ABOUT THE SIZE OF A PC MESS HALL.
I ALSO HAVE A SMALL COMPARTMENT OF MY OWN... BY BIGGEST ACCOMPLISHMENT
SO FAR WAS THE TRIP FROM SAN PEDRO DOWN HERE. GETTING OUT OF
CERRITOS CANNNEL WAS THE BIGGEST JOB.... THE WIND REALLY HAS
TO BE TAKEN INTO CONSIDERATION, NO DRAFT AND ALL FREEBOARD.
I MANAGED A MOORING TO A NEST DOWN HERE WITH NO DAMAGE.. POOR
BOB HAS TO BRING HIS DOWN HERE FROM SAN FRANCISCO. , WRITE MY
HOME ADD:

                                    AS EVER , WEB

A final note from Web Smith.

Epilogue

Looking back to the war years of World War II I wonder about the enthusiasm for military service among the people of my age. The startling reality that the United States had been attacked in its own backyard may have accounted for some of the unquestioned support for the military effort. But it seemed to go beyond sheer patriotism. In reviewing my wartime correspondence, I seem to have relished what I was doing. Most of my contemporaries, all men in their early 20's, were in the service. With few exceptions they rose to the challenge of the heavy responsibilities with which they were charged. They performed with competence. If they had doubts about their ability to do the job, those doubts were soon dispelled by events which required their attention and subsequent action. In the act of doing the job, of exercising the responsibilities, they gained confidence and the satisfaction of a job well done. They were not alone. Their neighbors, their friends, their colleagues from school or work, were in similar situations. They supported and identified with one another.

Camaraderie and a certain joie de vivre prevailed. There were times of loneliness but they were offset by the antics and good humor of compatible shipmates. There were times of fear but not dispair. The Navy had given us minimal training and thrown us into the fray with the hope and expectation that we could cope. By and large we did. To a large extent it was sink or swim, and we managed to swim. As we looked around we saw all of the others coping, so it didn't seem unusual for a 25 year old to be commanding a multi-million dollar ship with a crew of 72 men. When I successfully docked the ship for the first time, the crew cheered. Each time I fixed the position of the ship through starsights, it was a thrill. When the ship cut through monstrous waves I was exhilarated — and fortunately not seasick. It wasn't a case of proving yourself, but it was a maturing experience. There were no heroics.

There were times when we thought the war would never end. We wanted to go home but we were not paranoid about it. As much as I liked the work of the Navy I began to have an uneasy feeling that I was being cheated out of four years when I could have been getting on with my life and career. In retrospect the Navy experience was a rewarding four years of personal development in a wartime environment over which I had no control. There really wasn't a choice and I tried to make the best of it.

These observations are strictly my own. They reflect my experience, serving as a Naval Reserve Officer on small ships in the Pacific Theater of World War II. Those who became casualties of combat, those who suffered, and those who died may have had a more calloused or even a bitter attitude toward the Navy experience, but I doubt it. They too had a job to do and I suspect that they did it with spirit and a sense of responsibility.

About the Author

Jim and Dorothy Schultz as they appear today.

James R. Schultz is a native of Northwest Pennsylvania and graduated from Allegheny College in his hometown of Meadville. He entered Harvard Business School in the fall of 1941 and was there when the Japanese bombed Pearl Harbor on December 7. The day after the attack the Commandant of the First Naval Disctrict in Boston came to the campus and delivered a stirring address in which he encouraged students to volunteer for service in the United States Naval Reserve. Mr. Schultz was one of many who responded to the call. He was commissioned an Ensign in April 1942 and in May left to attend a sixty day Midshipmen's training program at Northwestern University. The Long Way Home is the story of his wartime experience.

After the war Mr. Schultz returned to Harvard and graduated with an M.B.A.. He and Dorothy Louise Koster were married a month later. They have three daughters, Linda Robinson, Margaret Blair, and Nancy Symons and five granddaughters, Laura, Emily and Chelsea Robinson, and Ashley and Rachel Symons. He pursued a career in personnel management and organization development with Kaiser Aluminum and Chemical Corporation and later entered the executive recruiting field where he served as Managing Director of the San Francisco office of SpencerStuart. Now retired, he and Mrs. Schultz reside in Lafayette, California where they are active in church and community affairs.

G L O S S A R Y

Armada   A fleet of warships

Battle bill   A posted list of assignments to battle stations aboard ship

Beachhead   A position gained by invading an enemy shore

Bow   The front part of a ship

Breech clout   A cloth worn to cover the loins

Bulkhead   An upright partition used to divide a ship into watertight and fireproof compartments

Carabao   A water buffalo

Catwalk   A narrow, elevated walk

Chautauqua (Travelling)   A travelling tent show that brought stage plays, lectures, and musical entertainment to small towns prior to 1933

Clipper   A sailing ship built for great speed, applied to the flying boats of Pan American Airways

Coastwatcher   A person operating behind enemy lines on Japanese held islands in WWII to provide information on ship, aircraft, and troop movements.

Coolie   An unskilled native laborer in Asia

Conn   The act or process of steering a vessel

Coxwain   One who steers a small boat

Flotilla   A small fleet of ships

Foxhole   A hole dug in the ground as protection from enemy gunfire

Galley   A ship's kitchen

Guerilla   A member of a small defensive force of irregular soldiers making surprise raids

Knot (nautical) A unit of speed, about 1.15 statute miles per hour

Midshipman   A student in training to be a naval officer

Periscope   An optical instrument which permits observation around or over an obstacle, used in submarines

Port   The left side of a ship as one faces forward.

Sampan   A small boat used on the waterways of the Orient

Schooner   A ship with two or more masts rigged fore and aft

Semaphore   Any visual signaling apparatus, including flags, lights, or mechanical arms

Sextant   An instrument for measuring the angular distance from the sun or a star to the horizon to determine a position at sea

Shrapnel   Fragments scattered by an exploding artillery shell

Skipper   The commanding officer of a ship

Sniper   One who shoots from a hidden position

Squall   A brief, violent windstorm, usually with heavy rain

Starboard   The right side of a ship as one faces forward

Steam fitter   One whose work is installing boillers, pipes, etc. in steam pressure systems

Stern   The back end of a ship

Strafed   Attacked by machine gun fire by low-flying aircraft

Wardroom   A dining room for commissioned officers

Yeoman   A petty officer assigned to clerical duty

Zero   A Japanese fighter plane used in WWII

I N D E X